BOBBY THOMPSON

A Private Audience

DAVE NICOLSON

D1264595

ISBN 1 901237 02 8
Printed and Published by TUPS Books
30, Lime St. Newcastle upon Tyne, NE1 2PQ
Tel. No: 0191 2330990 Fax: 0191 2330578

Typeset by Design 2 Print
5 Jubilee Terrace, Crawcrook, Tyne & Wear

ACKNOWLEDGEMENTS

I wish to thank the following people who have helped me with this book.

Keith and Michael Thompson, Elizabeth, Paddy and Rosie Fox, Joe Ging, Brian Shelley, Richard Kelly, Ken Pope (for many kindnesses), Ronnie Vaughan and Mark Lewis, Bobby Pattinson, Homer Michaelides, Father Cass, Ed Simmons (we nearly found those ladies), Corrinne Wilde, Helen Russell, Danny La Rue, David Jason, Simon Willis, Howard Thompson, Colin Faddy, Carol Donald, Billy Aynsley, John Larkin, Dave Wood, Mrs Starbuck, Pat Healy, Philip Jones, Tony Sands, Phil Penfold, Roy Hudd, Ken Dodd, Craig Douglas, Doreen Daglish and Lily Coates.

Lines from Bobby Thompson's recorded act are reproduced by permission of Dave Wood and Keith Thompson.

Finally, to Maureen, for her belief, patience and many hours of assistance.

Jacket design and photographs by Dave Nicolson (the Woodbine packet - Bobby Thompson's stage-prop for over 30 years - is reproduced by permission of the Imperial Tobacco Company and is not in any way an advert for smoking).

DEDICATION

This book is dedicated to my mother, Helen Reid, who gave me a lasting interest in variety theatre. I shall always remember how a dreary life could be transformed for two hours by a seat in the 'gods' and little figures upon a stage.

CONTENTS

FROM THE FAMILY   7
FOREWORD   8
INTRODUCTION   9
A LIFE   13

INTERVIEWS

BILLY AYNSLEY   25
BOBBY PATTINSON   27
PAT HEALY   31
LILY COATES   35
MICHAEL THOMPSON   38
KEITH THOMPSON   63
ED SIMMONS   99
RICHARD KELLY   104
JOE GING   117
MRS STARBUCK   126
PADDY FOX   129
PHILIP JONES   139
DANNY LA RUE   141
CRAIG DOUGLAS   142
DOREEN DAGLISH   145
BRIAN SHELLEY   147
FATHER CASS   162
TONY SANDS   165
DAVE WOOD   168
DAVID JASON   172
ROY HUDD   173
DAVE NICOLSON   174
PHIL PENFOLD   181
CORRINNE WILDE   183
MARK LEWIS   184
RONNIE VAUGHAN   185
HOMER MICHAELIDES   187

Bella Blahole remembered.

FROM THE FAMILY

During his lifetime and after his death, people have always wanted to do something or other on my dad. When my brother, Michael, and I agreed to be interviewed for this book, it was on the understanding that, above all, the finished product should be a true portrait of our father through our eyes and those of other people. To be perfectly honest, neither of us thought that a book could be put together.

Although we thought that we had nothing more to learn about him (how wrong we were) we realised the risk of a final picture which did not reflect Bobby Thompson's lovable public image. As the months rolled on, we learned many things about our father, mother and ourselves - some of which were painful to acknowledge.

Dave Nicolson's research led us to a welcome meeting with our half-sister, Beatrice (from dad's first marriage to Anna Marjoram.) Although she never had the chance to know Bobby Thompson as her father, Beatrice had been a missing piece of our family picture for many years.

As things have turned out, I am delighted with this book and somewhat relieved that far from altering the 'Little Waster's' image it has, warts and all, deepened and enhanced the public man and more importantly, for Michael and myself, our father. This book, like Bobby Thompson, will be a very hard act to follow.

Keith Thompson

1994

FOREWORD

Comics come in all shapes, sizes and styles - ranging from the clown in baggy trousers to the man in the well-cut suit. But they share one thing in common - the ability to make people laugh. To a comedian, there is nothing quite like the sound of laughter. To have an audience in uproar, to help them forget their everyday problems and worries, if only for an evening, is an experience to treasure.

The music hall has known many great comics: funsters who made audiences laugh performance after performance, year after year. Their humour remains timeless. Max Miller in his outrageous suits, the gentle understated comedy of Robb Wilton, the grotesque antics of Max Wall. Comedy craftsmen like Jimmy James, Sandy Powell, Arthur Askey and Tommy Cooper. And right up there with them in the Premier League is Bobby Thompson, Tyneside's own 'Little Waster'.

Like them, Bobby was a 'one-off', an emaciated figure crowned by a flat cap. He was the little man fighting back - cheeky, chauvinistic, yet vulnerable and appealing. He made no secret of his shortcomings - or ours. Many people associate Andy Capp with Bobby's stage character, but 'The Little Waster' had warmth and vulnerability and you always had the feeling that his missus would have the last word!

With his talent, plus a posh accent, he could have been a top of the bill act throughout the UK and gained a huge following on television during the Fifties and Sixties. But he loved the North-East and its people too much and they loved him because he was their own.

Bobby was that rarest of comedians, a man who could make his fellow comics laugh - even if we had to travel to the North-East for the pleasure. 'The Little Waster' he may have been, but you never wasted your money when you went to one of his shows. You were guaranteed to come out limp with laughter, and I can think of no finer tribute.

KEN DODD

INTRODUCTION

Friday afternoons in 1951 were hectic in my small area of Newcastle's West End. After school and a bolted tea, the race began. Pop bottles were found and returned for their deposits, and old clothes (particularly woollens) were sold to second-hand shops or rag-and-bone men if they happened to be in the back lane at tea-time. Normally, these street entrepreneurs were out in force, enticing kids to part with their mothers' old clothes. In return, they were given a set of three coloured marbles or a highly-prized goldfish. The dazzling fish was a novelty to post-war children who had only ever seen colourless sticklebacks from the Leazes or Exhibition Parks.

The purpose our mother set us to on these Friday afternoons was to raise a few shillings for bus fares and first house seats in the 'gods' at the Grand Theatre, Byker, Newcastle upon Tyne. My mother had a deep-seated love of variety shows, obtained from accompanying her father, a scene-shifter, when he worked at the Empire Theatre, Newcastle. She had been raised by her father in relative poverty, leaving school at fourteen to go into service. The 'means test' men calling, wearing second-hand clothes, and generally scrimping to make-do were a way of her childhood life that had to be borne. Her release was a live show and the working-class humour that recognised not only the inescapable plight of working class, but also laughed at the frailty and weaknesses of its characters.

As children, we sometimes wondered whether our traumatic Fridays were worthwhile. There would be an unpleasant scene when we arrived home to a father who would 'play war'. He didn't like coming home from the shipyard (on pay night) to an oven tea, no wife, and having to fill up the zinc bath himself for his weekly fireside scrub. We rarely understood the theatre humour or why everyone laughed, and would, given the chance, have chosen the pictures. Our mother was transported as tears of laughter reddened her face (for which we got the blame all the way home.) She seemed to lose her timidity and we lived in weekly fear that she would embarrass us by getting up on stage to show her underwear for a prize of ten shillings. There were plenty of other takers and she never did join the queue, but temptation must have been great. Such a sum would have meant the difference between struggling with her housekeeping for the next week or managing comfortably.

Top of the bill on these Friday nights at The Grand was usually a pint-sized comedian called Bobby Thompson. He talked of his wife, his in-laws, his son Tadger, their life, debts and neighbours. I can't remember whether or not he carried his Woodbine cigarette packet of five then - we were too far back and not interested in the detail - but he stood there and made people laugh and laugh.

Looking back, he was making them laugh at themselves, and at what life had handed out, through his own inadequate stage character. He met the old music hall yardstick 'of the people for the people'. Years later, Bobby Thompson was to tell me that when you have nothing then there is only despair or laughter. To him there wasn't a choice. The seed had been sown in my brain and I have stayed with his humour for forty years.

As the years passed, Bobby Thompson's name alone could produce laughter. Stage clothes were a sloppy jumper (gansey) truncated plus-fours, flat cap and slippers. Occasionally, he would wear an ill-fitting army uniform. The act had only three or four minor variations and new jokes were rare and introduced almost nervously. His eyes could be made to look into each other and there was invariably a song at the end. This was usually amateurish, but served to further endear him to his audience. Thousands of 'Go-As-You-Please' club turns and members of the public felt that they too could tell a joke and certainly sing like Bobby.

I didn't lose touch - there were his radio shows. I used to see him on the coast train occasionally, always dapper, polite and quiet - unless he wanted to smoke and some one mentioned that he was in a non-smoking carriage. Once, I sat opposite him from Monkseaton to Newcastle, trying to watch without being rude, as he spoke soothingly and gently to occupy a fractious child who had been driving his parents, and me, to distraction.

After the Brooks Brothers court appearance for non-payment of a clothing debt, someone, who knew of my interest, told me he was working temporarily in the shirts and ties department of a gents' outfitters in Grainger Street, Newcastle. I found him at the third attempt and clearly recall pretending to select a tie while watching him. Unfortunately, we were the only two in that department and he kept an eye on my movements, walking behind the long wooden counters to keep me in his vision. After five or ten minutes of this silent manoeuvring, I left the shop (without a purchase) with my curiosity satisfied. When I reached eighteen, and joined the Club and Institute Union, my contact was more regular as I travelled to any club where he was appearing. We finally met in November 1980 when he gave me an interview at his home and then let me accompany him when he was working.

The Geordie dialect (before 'Auf Wiedersehn Pet' and 'Spender') prevented general recognition, although he was known nationally in the business. National exposure happened towards the end of his life when it wasn't really important and I believe that it never mattered to him. Just the sight of him walking on to a Northern theatre or club in his cap and gansey could make the audiences laugh and anticipate like Pavlovian dogs. One old man turned to me in a club, after Bobby had made the usual entrance, and told me that it always puzzled him how he could laugh afresh every time he came to see Bobby Thompson - even though he had been watching the same old act for years.

His humour, with its central theme of debt and pretension, was timeless, even though the settings were more appropriate to his own prime time of the Thirties to late Fifties. When the North-East people became more affluent and tried to cast off the cloth-cap-and-pigeons image, they made no attempt to discard the sign-post to their roots in the form of Bobby Thompson. Like all great music hall entertainers, despite his magic aura, he belonged to them. Mentally, they kept him in his own time capsule, to make them laugh and remind them of what they were and where they came from. For his part, he never wanted to be anywhere else. Speak to any North-Easterner who is acquainted with Bobby Thompson's humour and they know him and feel at ease with him, even when the jokes are at their expense. He made fun of them through himself and they willingly laughed at both.

This book was never intended to be a biography nor, in my opinion, could it have been one. Bobby Thompson was not an international nor even a national figure, but he did personify the humour and spirit of the North-East of England. Most of his showbusiness life was well documented in his home area because, as its greatest celebrity for nearly forty years, Bobby Thompson was always newsworthy. For much of his life, he lived a repetitive private and public existence in a goldfish bowl - never trying to get away - and in turn observing the North-East people, with the sharp comedian's eye, as they passed by.

As for all of us, there were private sides to his life, only witnessed by a small number. Nearly everyone who was related or close to him, and could be contacted, was invited to take part. Perhaps for some, like his daughter and relatives, it was too late and they had never really known him anyway. For others, recollections were painful and to remain private - perhaps to be brought out elsewhere in their own good time.

In the five years that it took to put this book together, it became very clear that every one of his family and private associates got fragments of Bobby. Few, if any, got near it all. The key players are all here, and, if nothing else, their recorded memories reveal how Bobby Thompson played to his private audience over many years. Unlike his club and theatre audiences, many of them were not free to walk out on the show and, unlike the professional entertainer, he was not free to choose his venue and audience. This book collects their memories of how he played to them and affected their lives - the private man and his private audience.

A LIFE

Robert Michael Thompson was born the last of seven children to John and Mary Thompson (née Kane) on November 18, 1911, at 4, The Staithes, Penshaw, County Durham. On the same day, Bobby's grandmother was buried. His mother had more than a full-time job being at home, and his father worked as a deputy pit overman at North Biddick Colliery. Of his six brothers and sisters, Jimmy was the eldest, followed by Kate, Mary, Rosina, Albert and Jack.

Large families in working-class communities were regarded as a mixed blessing. A burden, often due to ignorance and drunken stupidity, on one hand and on the other, comparative affluence at working age if the family was mainly male and in full-time work. Before the First World War, girls were expected to help at home after leaving school at the age of 14, perhaps taking in washing or going into the service of better-off people. Albert, Jack and Jimmy followed their father down the pit.

Often, ignorance of family planning and stupidity were not factors. With good Catholic families like the Thompsons, the 'Father' would often nudge long-married couples, where the woman was still of child-bearing age, 'not to hold back'. Having borne six children, perhaps young Robert Michael was the final straw in a hard life of making ends meet, making do, washing, and the constant fear of injury (and loss of income) in the pits to husbands and sons.

In most mining communities and factory towns, life ran to similar patterns. Shoes and clothing would usually be second-hand, patched, repaired and not guaranteed to fit. Things were handed down as a matter of course, and very often the youngest went without or had the odd new item as a rare alternative. New clothing was more likely if there was a large gap between the last arrival and the rest of the family. Cross-dressing was common, and heaven help the lad who was unfortunate enough to be the youngest child in a family of sisters. Some kids went to school with little more than some underwear and a towel pinned around them.

Pit work was long and dangerous - with little come-back on the tight grip of mine owners or their safety measures. Miners took the coal dust home with them, both in their lungs and on their bodies. Apart from wiping hands and face to eat, bathing was usually saved for a Friday night. This would usually take place in a large tin bath set in front of a coal fire which heated the water. Social life centred around church, shops, public houses, workingmen's clubs and the two-penny village hop. Dominoes, cards, pitch-and-toss were both pastimes and threats to the week's housekeeping money. Credit clubs, street money-lenders and the pawnbrokers were expensive but necessary lifelines. Allotments were common, providing room for a pigeon loft as well as vegetables and poultry for the table. There were many areas of greater deprivation than the rural mining area of Penshaw, County Durham, into which Bobby Thompson was born. Industrial towns were a worse environment, and without the compensation of green fields and fresh air.

In 1911, poverty in the working class was a normal state rather than an exception. You cannot feel deprived of shoes and steak if everyone else is shoeless and feeding on bread and jam and sheep's head broth ('leave the eyes in, they'll see us through the week'.)

Children, as ever, made their own amusement in the countryside around them, with home-made tops and whips or stick and hoop from the Co-op butter barrel (you didn't have to be able to afford the butter to get the hoop, but it helped.) Kicking a rusty tin block around, or rides on hay bogies were some of the other amusements.

Bobby's first brush with authority started at St. Joseph's School, Washington, County Durham, with the school board 'wagman' and the headmistress, Miss Downey. The family had moved in 1915 to New Bridge Street, Penshaw. By the time he was eight years old, four years later, Bobby had lost both parents. They died in their forties within a year of each other.

Bringing up little Bobby now fell to his sister, Rosina, who lived at Wagon Way Terrace, Fatfield, and Bobby transferred to the school there.

When Rosina married in 1922, he went to live with Kate at New Penshaw where he finished his schooling. By all accounts, his nine years of education were uneventful - save for the fact that, being a very small boy, he learned and applied humour as his best defence from potential bullies. A contemporary remembers 'Little Tonka', as he was known, being well liked, although he was neither a great scholar nor too bright outside of school. 'Tonka' wore glasses with one lens for his squint, made his friends laugh ('too funny to be taken seriously'), and pinched whatever he could, like everyone else in the gang. He never got into serious trouble and seemed devoid of malice.

Apart from the children of publicans and shopkeepers (the butcher's son had meat in his sandwiches), most of his fellow pupils would have the same background and circumstances as himself. The careful observation of his own class, and total identification with it, was eventually his act and no other.

At Fatfield, he developed his taste for performing in public when he and another lad went around as 'guisers'. The duo, dressed in odd clothes and with blackened faces, sang from door to door and in pubs if they could get in. Bobby's speciality was "My Child You Have No Mother Now" - a real tear-jerker and halfpenny earner. His highlight around this period was winning a local talent contest at The Gem Theatre, Penshaw. This time "My Child You Have No Mother Now" won him a gold watch and sharpened his appetite for entertaining people. The audience gave their sympathy to the pathetic little urchin with no shoes, patched pants and a gansey, who sang a nice soprano. The rewards of fame were short-lived. Mr Jones's pawnshop, in Washington, got the watch for ten shillings a few days later.

When he left school at 14, it was pit work or nothing. With a guardian sister looking after him, money was an absolute necessity and so Bobby, like his father and brothers before him, started at North Biddick Pit. He joined his three brothers - Jimmy who was a 'shuvver-in' of the tubs of coal, Albert, a horse-keeper, and Jack a datal worker. Bobby started as a 'coupler-on lad', linking the tubs of coal together. He never forgot that first day which started at four in the afternoon and ended at midnight. Too tired to eat, he slept till two the next afternoon and then went down again at four. His wage was seven shillings and nine pence a week.

During his teens, he continued to sing and play harmonica, often doing a turn in a pub or club for a few shillings. He learned to dance and liked the ladies and, in turn, some of them took to him. Whatever he lacked in formal education as a young man, he had an agile mind and a good head for figures. His reputation for dominoes was widespread and often provided a supplement to his wages.

In 1931, when he was nineteen, Biddick Colliery closed and although he was offered a transfer to the Glebe Colliery nearby, he never took it up. He was now without a regular job. During the next ten years, he claimed dole or did general labouring jobs on building sites or in factories. In the evenings and on Sundays, he performed in and out of various concert parties like Bobby Docherty's Washington Bright Stars and Billy Bankhead's Bluebird Harmonica Band. He sang, danced, played the harmonica, and occasionally told jokes. At one point, he tried his hand at being a female impersonator.

It was during a spell with the Washington Bright Stars in 1932 that Bobby (encouraged by his boss who was trying to fill a programme gap) tried his hand at solo comedy at the Silksworth Buffs Club in County Durham. It was not a success and the club steward advised him: 'The lads is restless, Bobby', and not to try again in the second half.

The Bluebird Band brought a different experience, for it was with them that he made his first radio broadcast in 1934 on a programme called 'Pit People'. The band, which consisted of two accordion players, including Gillie Scott who was blind, five mouth organists and a guitarist, received two guineas. Back then, you could buy a dozen harmonicas for twelve shillings. Undaunted by his comedy debut at Silksworth Buffs, he played harmonica and told jokes with the Bluebird Band.

If he hadn't a casual job, and to supplement his seven-and-sixpence dole money, he would pick coal off the slag heaps and sell it from his bike to those who could afford to buy. At night, he cleaned his dirty shoes and went dancing or to see variety acts at nearby theatres. During this period, he moved in and out of a variety of lodgings in the Washington area.

In 1934, Bobby met Anna Marjoram at a dance and married her, after a formal courtship, on April 11, 1936, in the Parish church of Howarth, County Durham. Relatives remember Bobby, who stood around 5 feet 3 inches, proudly bringing Anna, who was much taller and very slim, to tea at sister Kate's on Sundays. They had one child, a daughter, Beatrice, who was born on February 16, 1938, at 11, Quarry Row, Usworth, County Durham. However, the marriage lasted a very short time and they split up not long after the baby was born. Bobby claimed that they were unsuited in temperament, and his lifestyle of concert parties cannot have helped to create domestic stability. Wife, Anna, and daughter, Beatrice, do not appear to have received any contact or maintenance after the separation.

By 1940, Bobby was seeing Phyllis Coates (Born October 2, 1910), the daughter of Alf Coates, a full-time colliery official and local Methodist lay preacher. Bobby had known her from his days in lodgings when she had occasionally acted as driver to the Washington Bright Stars concert party. Phyllis was the black sheep of her family and weighed in at about sixteen stones. She towered above Bobby by six or seven inches and people recall her riding her motorbike with little Bobby perched on the pillion seat.

Bobby, now aged 29, received his call-up papers in early February, 1941, at 'Fern-Lea', Heworth Road, his Washington lodgings. On February 27, Private Robert Michael Thompson No 3606184 was posted to No. 18 Initial Training Company of the Border Regiment (embodied Territorial Army) at their Durham Hill Camp outside Carlisle. Phyllis followed him and got herself a job as an ambulance driver. Progress was not fast and on September 7, 1942, he was posted to the 68th Primary Training Company. December 16, 1943, saw Bobby posted to the No. 2 Army

Selection Centre before being discharged on January 5, 1944, because he ceased to fulfil army medical requirements. During his three year stint in the army, 'Little Enoch', as he became known, continued to do odd jobs just as he had done in civvy street.

Following his discharge, he lived with Phyllis in Victoria Cottage, Great Corby, Carlisle, and tried his hand at being a postman. Although riding around on a bike was nothing new for him, he was sacked (according to Bobby) for not delivering mail to remote farm-houses.

Anna divorced Bobby on September 17, 1945, and married Henry Wilson in early 1946. Bobby and Phyllis wed at the Border Register Office, Carlisle, on October 4, 1945, two days after Phyllis's thirty-fifth birthday. The marriage certificate records the groom's occupation as 'Variety Artist'.

In 1946, Bobby and Phyllis returned to Tyneside, took a room in Newcastle and drew the dole. Ration books were still in use, the NHS was still a gleam in the Labour Party's eye and two World Wars had taken and used the cream of two generations. Post-war rebuilding and defence programmes gave birth to a measure of working-class prosperity, even in the North-East of England.

Club and pub work kept some money coming in for a while and he changed his name to Bobby Corby (after Great Corby). By the late Forties, although his reputation was growing, he had to take a 'regular' job as a can-lad (tea-maker, message-goer and bet-placer) wherever he could. By this time, Phyllis had a son, Robert Michael, who was born on November 15, 1948, and home, by then, was a one-room flat in Barley Mow, County Durham. In the evenings, he performed with Bobby Dawson's Five Chesters. A second son, Keith, was born on June 29, 1950, and the family moved into a rented house at 20, Lowfield Crescent, Great Lumley, County Durham.

By 1951, Bobby had joined a stage show called the 'Merry Magpies' run by E. J. Hinge, a Northern impresario, who owned the Grand Theatre,

Byker, in Newcastle and the Civic Theatre, Darlington. Here, Bobby was on wages and the show enjoyed a 70 week run at the Grand. This successful show extended the life of a fine old variety theatre which had played host to the finest artists in music hall. During this run, Bobby had his last spell of full-time employment as a labourer from March 5, 1951, to December 28, 1951, at the Royal Ordnance Factory, Birtley, County Durham. The decision to leave the additional security of a full-time job was fuelled in November of that year. Bobby's personal boat had sailed up the river when he successfully auditioned for BBC Radio's 'Wot Cheor Geordie'. He was a success and Mr Hinge increased his wages. For the next six years, the 'Merry Magpies' toured theatres around the North of England, complemented by the continued success of Bobby on radio with follow-up shows like 'Bob's Your Uncle'. Bobby Thompson made a very good living right through the 1950s. BBC Radio money may not have been much, but the prestige was enormous and boosted an artist's drawing power in variety theatre (particularly in the pantomime season) and clubs.

There is the possibility that Bobby became a father for the fourth time on July 28, 1956. At a private nursing home in Jesmond, Newcastle, a son, Anthony, was born to a young dancer. The affair had been an 'open' one and, by all accounts, the lady made most of the running. The mother wanted to keep her son, but had to give into pressure from her own mother and part with the boy. At the young mother's request, Anthony was adopted by a show business couple in Cumbria and she returned to her parents home in Yorkshire.

In 1958, BBC Television had made severe inroads into the entertainment industry provided by variety acts on radio and stage, but it was left to commercial television to really signal the end. That year, Bobby received an offer that no comedian at that time could refuse - a contract, for sixteen of his own shows to begin in March 1959, from the newly-formed Tyne Tees Television company. Bobby enjoyed a successful pantomime season from December 1958 until January 1959 as Wishee Washee in 'Aladdin', with the South African singer Eve Boswell, at Newcastle's Empire Theatre - then turned his attention to the TV run.

'Meet the Thompson family and their friends at home and in the club. A new series featuring the Little Waster himself' was the TV guide's invitation to potential viewers of the first 'Bobby Thompson Show'. Predictably, in view of his popularity in the area served by the new TV station, and the novelty of having an alternative to BBC in the form of a commercial channel, the first show (transmitted live on Channel 8 at 9.30pm on Monday, March 16, 1959) was very well received. It topped the Television Audience Measurement (TAM) ratings, beating the likes of 'Wagon Train', 'Take Your Pick' and 'Emergency Ward 10'. His next two or three shows maintained popularity, but after that it was downhill all the way for the rest of the sixteen week run. After the fourth show, they didn't bother to provide the usual plot synopsis in 'The Viewer'. The first two shows used material provided by Bobby and Phyllis, but they could not possibly have provided for sixteen half-hour shows. The programme details show that for fourteen of the shows (starting with the third one) two professional scriptwriters were employed. One of them was Dan Douglas and the other was Lisle Willis - who had written very successfully for Bobby's radio shows. However, the best efforts of Willis, Douglas and everyone concerned (not to mention the weekly changes of set director) could not halt the show's rapid decline. One of the 'True or False' quiz questions in 'The Viewer' TV guide asked whether or not Somerset Maugham was Bobby Thompson's scriptwriter. For all the difference it would have made, he might as well have been.

The Tyne Tees Television series took Bobby away from his standard routines and placed him on the foreign soil of a sketch format with up and coming producer, Philip Jones. Over the years, many reasons have been put forward for the show's overall failure. Insufficient research to test Bobby Thopmpson's suitability for a transfer to TV; a lack of guidance from the production team; Bobby's lack of versatility; unsuitable scripts; poor casting for support roles and the inexperience of all concerned - they have all had an airing. The truth is probably an amalgam of all these factors, but hindsight is a wonderful tool for analysis. Whatever the apportionment of blame, when the last show went out on June 29, Bobby Thompson's career was badly damaged.

Fortunately, he and his agent, Fred Rout, had contracts which gave him good work until the end of the pantomime season in January 1960. He continued to headline at Northern theatres, but audiences weren't flocking in as before. The Newcastle Moss Empire Theatre's production of 'Cinderella', which began in December 1959, gave Bobby's Buttons character the chance to shine and he enjoyed a successful run. However, it was only a temporary stay of the inevitable deep trough which had already affected his life. It was during this pantomime run that Phyllis took over the managerial reins from Freddy Rout. Both Bobby and Phyllis liked their drink in considerable quantities, but after the television debacle he hit the ale with a vengeance and the money, from a financially successful year, flowed from his fingers. Only the bookie and the publican were laughing now. After the 1959/60 panto run, there was no work for three months. He then worked cabaret clubs in Doncaster, Rotherham and Sheffield. By the middle of 1960, apart from an odd week here and there, good theatre work had all but dried up and he returned to the North-East clubs to start again and make a living for the family.

In June 1960, he faced the Inland Revenue Commissioners at Sunderland. They wanted him for £900 in respect of two tax-years, 1957-59, but the money was gone. A Gateshead Court appearance on October 18, 1960, saw him back on the public carpet and sealed his fall. In a brief personal appearance, he admitted that he owed Brooks Brothers (Tailors) of Chester-le-Street the sum of £19. 5s. for clothing. Bobby had bought an overcoat, a suit, a shirt and vest from their shop costing a total of £35 5s, but had only paid them £16. He was ordered to pay off the debt at £2 a month. He made the excuses of Phyllis's ill health and his low earnings. Several supporters offered to pay his debt. His wife's health was not an excuse, as Phyllis had developed heart trouble after the television flop.

December 1960 to January 1961 saw Bobby return to Gateshead Magistrates Court. This time the plot could well have been taken from a Bobby Thompson script. Two brothers stood accused of stealing a £20 carpet from Phyllis. She had hired them to collect some furniture and carpets, from storage in Birtley, and bring them to her home in Gateshead. She did not check the goods when they were unloaded, but later found a length of carpet missing. The carpet was found by police in a Gateshead second-hand shop. Bobby had accompanied the brothers to Birtley and had spent four hours with them in a pub. One of the men claimed that Bobby Thompson had asked him if he wished to buy the goods, subject to Phyllis's approval. Phyllis had not agreed, but it was decided that after most of the goods had been unloaded the man should buy the remainder for £10. The carpet was among these goods and he took it not knowing that Phyllis did not intend to sell it. The case against the brothers was dismissed.

On March 15, 1961, Bobby appeared before Gateshead Magistrates Court again, this time for failing to pay National Insurance stamps amounting to £21 14s 1d. He was fined £10 and ordered to pay the arrears within twenty-one days.

Drink, problems with the tax-man, National Insurance contributions and missing carpets apart, Bobby Thompson had a family to support. Most nights, having slept off the lunch-time session, he headed for any club within a fifteen-mile radius which was running a 'Go-As-You-Please' evening. Here he would pick up a few pints and, if he was placed in the talent competition, a few pounds or shillings. Sometimes he would win, but many times he came home empty-handed and out of pocket on his fares. Third billing in Sunderland Empire's 'Mother Goose' pantomime, in December 1961, was the high-light of a poor year.

Towards the end of 1962, after an appearance at Balmbra's Music Hall in Newcastle, he began to get reasonable club bookings, but was notorious for his unreliability. If one club booked him for £4 and another offered ten shillings more, he would take the better price and never tell the first club that he was pulling out. He was still drinking and the pressure of Phyllis's illness didn't help.

In 1966, he met a young agent, Brian Shelley, who was just starting up. It was Brian who sorted him out and in doing so made Bobby

Thompson achieve his true potential and earning power for the next nineteen years. He had been down for three years and out of the big earners' league for seven years. For Bobby, it must have all seemed like a lifetime, for the bitterness of those years never left him. Phyllis lived to see his full comeback, but died on April 25, 1967.

Variety theatre had been moribund since the early Sixties, but the successful partnership with Brian Shelley saw his clubland earnings rise to £500 a night; a pantomime season for which he received £2,500-a-week for simply doing a twelve-minute spot at each performance; a best selling LP; a successful London debut at the Wimbledon Theatre; a 'Wogan' appearance and a Palladium show offer.

Only a Southern accent and national stardom could have brought more. Such was the consistency of his popularity (and his appetite for seven-nights-a-week work) that, in terms of earnings, he made the careers of many successful national comedians look pale by comparison. It is said that Arthur Askey had once called him 'the best English comic of this century' - certainly no-one in the North of England had the slightest doubt. For thirteen of those golden years, he was lovingly looked after by his housekeeper, Lottie Tate. Lottie's death hit him very hard: they had been a married couple in all but name. Bobby had success and money, but he also had loneliness. An engagement to Lottie's widowed sister, Mary Douglas (who refused to become his housekeeper), followed, but the romance foundered. On December 31, 1982, he got married, for the third time, to his housekeeper, Eleanor Cicely (Cissie) Palmer, a retired cook.

After his split with Brian Shelley in 1985, Bobby, at 73 years of age, was handled by the Lewis Vaughan Agency, but this switch coincided with his declining powers of co-ordination and delivery.

The last few years were embarrassing for him and his faithful audiences, but they too knew the score and were kind to him even if they didn't go to see him again. Empty tables and chairs in his beloved clubs told him the harsh truth. Even the Examiner at his bankruptcy hearing in 1986 for a tax bill of £137,000 was properly kind and considerate.

Having lost the real company of an audience, his feeling of loneliness and isolation intensified. He just couldn't break the love and habit of a lifetime - his driving need to be up there in the light, controlling the mood of his audience and working. Betting on dogs and horses had long lost their excitement. Now the Casino Royale and their roulette wheel provided his nightly stage and focal point.

Bobby died of Myocardial Infarction and Emphysema at 1.30am on Saturday, April 16, 1988, at Preston Hospital, North Shields. His sons, Keith and Michael, had stayed at his bedside throughout the night. He was survived by the boys, two grandchildren and wife Cissie (who died on April 13, 1995). A Requiem Mass was celebrated at St Mary's RC Church, Cullercoats, on April 20, followed by a service a Whitley Bay Crematorium.

The Times honoured him with an obituary and thousands turned out to pay their last respects. He had never fostered a close relationship with his fellow professionals, but would have been delighted at their final tributes which were delivered in his own style. His fellow comedians, in true showbusiness tradition, told jokes as they waited for the cortege, which had been delayed. Two of their one-liners summed up Bobby Thompson and his North-East spirit more than any words from the Church:

'He's late because he found out that there's another funeral after this and he wants to go on last!'

'He's decided to go to the church up the road... they offered him ten bob more!'

BILLY AYNSLEY

My brother, Jack, knew Bobby Thompson well from their schooldays, but my first real dealings with him were back in 1933 when Jack, Bobby and I were members of Billy Bankhead's Harmonica Band. There were actually two bands, senior and junior, and we were in the juniors. The band had eight members. There were five mouth-organists: me, Jack, Bobby, Larry Greener and Billy Bankhead Senior. Gillie Scott (who was blind) and Billy Bankhead Junior both played accordion and Tommy Greener was our guitarist.

Our mouth-organs were all Bluebird models, made by Hohner of Germany, and that's why we were often called Billy Bankhead's Bluebird Harmonica Band. Bobby was single at that time and living in various digs around the area. For a while he stayed with a Mrs Deakin at Waterside, Washington. He was a good band member, but never one of the lads outside of it. We used to rehearse on a Friday night in a room at the Ferryboat Inn in (Old) Fatfield. Being part of a band we used to try to dress ourselves smartly, but although Bobby was a very keen musician he would turn himself out a bit scruffy and had to be told to smarten himself up.

After rehearsal, my mother used to put on a bit of a supper for us, usually ham with pease pudding, and Bobby would come back with us to eat and make music with the family in our front room. For a little bloke he could certainly shift the food. In this area he wasn't greatly liked and was regarded by many people as a bit of a scrounger who would neither work nor want. He borrowed a suit from me, in the Billy Bankhead days, when we played on the wireless (BBC Newcastle) for their 'In Town Tonight' programme in 1934. I never got it back from him. As it was only one of two good suits that I possessed at that time, this has always stuck in my mind, but that's the way he was. On another occasion, he borrowed someone's pushbike and crashed it.

People were pleased when he got on, but many didn't know what all the fuss was about. He wasn't the kind of man who kept in touch and I saw him rarely after he left the band in 1936. When I joined the Army in 1938, we lost touch completely. In his successful radio days, he gave the impression of being a little better than local people as he had 'got on'.

His irreverence didn't endear him to local people either. There is a strong Catholic population around here in Washington and on one occasion, I think it was at the Stella Maris Club, he looked at a picture of 'The Last Supper' hanging in the foyer and asked: 'Is that the Committee then?'

Don't worry about what you owe. Let them worry that wants it off you.

The dole is my shepherd, I shall not work.

BOBBY PATTINSON

I knew Bobby Thompson when I was a child. My mother and father were both in the entertainment business. My dad, Bob, was a booker of club turns and my mother, Ruby, had her own concert party, The Optimists, in which she was a comedienne.

At breakfast time on Sunday mornings, Bobby would regularly cycle through to our Gateshead house, from his home in Lumley, to see if my dad had any bookings for him. This would be around 1938/9 when I was three or four years old. I remember him as a gentle man that I liked - he was some twenty three years older than me - and I would sit on his knee while he ate breakfast. In those days he was a female impersonator. Like most drag acts the humour was broad and, as the clubs were rather narrow-minded, he was a hard act for my dad to book. My mother was top-dog, comedy-wise, with her party. Bobby liked to work with her whenever possible, but she could leave him standing as a comic talent.

Although he was gentle and often kindly, I could never understand his attitude towards other performers, never allowing or giving them any credit. This I found pathetic, but put it down to his insecurity. Why he was so insecure I never knew, as he had tremendous talent. Even when he was giving praise, he appeared insincere. He didn't encourage new talent at all and I had first-hand experience of that. It was in 1957, when I appeared with my concert party, The Skyliners, at the Bank Top Club, Throckley, Newcastle upon Tyne, and Bobby Thompson was in the audience. That particular night was tremendous for us as far as the audience was concerned and my own comedy act went enormous. After the show, Bobby came into the dressing-room and said: 'Great show, lads, you were marvellous.' He then took me to one side and said: 'Bobby, son, divvent de the comedy, stick to the singin.' The other two Skyliners, Alec Davison and Jimmy Coldwell were furious. I never learned anything from him. Everything I learned came from my mother, who was one of the greatest comediennes in the world.

Bobby's series at Tyne Tees Television in 1959 ruined him. Philip Jones was the producer and I believe Bobby wasn't directed properly. It was a cheap budget show in the very early days of Tyne Tees, badly written and badly directed. They used contract Cockney players like Harold Berens and Len Marten to play Geordie parts and other players like Colin Prince and Jack Haig. They were all OK individually, but they simply didn't fit into a Bobby Thompson sketch. The show didn't give him a chance. Bobby and Phyllis's behaviour did not help matters. They used to drink a lot and I remember in one of the episodes they had Pearl Carr and Teddy Johnson as the musical guests. Phyllis could be quite loud-mouthed and abusive and I heard that the Johnsons were quite taken aback by her behaviour in the studio foyer one evening.

When he left radio for television he was very big, but after the TV fiasco his reputation really hit the bottom and I am led to believe that he became a heavy drinker. At Tyne Tees, he missed the guidance of a strong mentor like he had in Richard Kelly at BBC Radio. He would let people down right, left and centre with bookings. He was amoral rather than immoral. I remember being in a pub, in 1962, when Ronnie Teasdale booked him for the Bedlington Terrier pub at 22/6d for a Wednesday night spot. Fifteen minutes later he had accepted a booking from someone else for the Stanley Victoria Club, because they were paying him half a crown more. When I asked him why he had taken the second job, he told me that the extra would pay for his bus fares 'and a couple of drinks for me and wor lass.' The sad part was that he didn't tell the Bedlington Terrier. I asked him what he was doing the following Wednesday. He said: 'Nothing,' and I suggested that he should have done the Bedlington Terrier and put the Stanley Victoria in for the following Wednesday. He said: 'I could be dead by then.' He had no conscience on these matters and was never a good businessman. Behavioural problems like these certainly didn't help his image. He could never drive a car and used to select singers for his club acts who could transport him about and who he didn't have to pay very much.

I never ever saw him as a rival, even in the North-East, but regarded him as a friend - even though from time to time people told me he didn't have a good word for me. They would add, too, that he was probably jealous. I don't know, maybe something rankled. He was based in the North-East (and worked within it for virtually the whole of his career) whereas I have topped the bill at major theatres and night-clubs throughout the English-speaking world. I have carried out three separate Las Vegas engagements, appeared widely on TV and succeeded as a businessman. Bobby was a good comic, a great comic, but there were others in the North-East who were comparable, like The Dixielanders and Walter Gee.

Bobby always wanted to be last on the bill - no matter what show he was on. Bobby interpreted this as the top of the bill spot. Most of the North-East comics were content to go on in any order, do their spot and then have a drink and watch the others. I was always prepared to let him go on last on any bill that we were both on, as I was confident in my abilities to go out and do the show I wanted to do. He was never one of the lads with the other comics, perhaps because he was quite a bit older. It's a great pity really because the others respected him and it could have made his life happier.

People say that he did a great deal for charity, but he always wanted a £100 fee to appear. In my experience, he never gave his services completely free for charity, although others may be able to say that he did.

Over the years, I have given him bookings and he appeared at my club, The Geordie Lad, in Benton, Newcastle upon Tyne. He wasn't as successful as I had hoped and in the 1981 December season I had to cancel sixteen shows. Brian Shelley bought The Geordie Lad in April 1982 and put Bobby in as the resident attraction. I had advised him against it, but he felt that Bobby could draw audiences for a week's stint - 'The Bobby Thompson Music Hall Show'. My logic was that if I couldn't fill it with Bobby in December then there was little chance of him filling it through May, June, July and August. I don't think that it was a success and while I don't actually know, I think it could have been the reason for the break-up of their partnership. Once again, it must be appreciated that 1982 was the beginning of the demise of the entertainment industries in Britain. It was the year when the few remaining variety theatres closed together with cabaret clubs, and workingmen's clubs began to suffer. There were some 8,000 cabaret clubs in the late 60s and early 70s. By the early 80s, they had started to close and the slump was world-wide.

He was a tremendous, good, clean comic - never blue - with topical lines like the Red Adair stories, and all credit due to him for making such a remarkable comeback through the Beverley Artistes Agency and manager Brian Shelley's guidance. He became clean and always immaculately turned out after his comeback and, although Lottie Tate had a hand in that, it was always the style of the man.

Aa said to the undertaker: 'Excuse me, Mr Wilson, how much would ye mak is a coffin for?'
He said: 'Thou's not very big, Bobby, - £14.'
Aa said: 'Lend's two and charge the wife £16.'

Why this would be a nudist camp if all the women took their catalogue stuff off.

PAT HEALY

As a young man, I was a hairdresser by trade living in Essex. I met a Newcastle girl, who was working at a local hospital, and moved up there with her to get married. Hairdressing at Bainbridges, Newcastle, paid me £3 per week in 1939/40, and in a good week I made £5 with tips. I had always been a singer and loved to entertain. My first real paid bookings were as an Irish tenor at Madame Brown's Metropole Cafe in Northumberland Street, Newcastle (later to become Michael's night club.) I used to entertain at their afternoon tea dances for a fee of ten shillings and my tea. Anything to do with showbusiness fascinated me and I loved to be part of it. Today, I'm still entertaining and as keen as ever.

The big force in North-East showbusiness at that time was E.J. Hinge, who owned cinemas, theatres and ran a large showbusiness agency. In the late Forties, I was spotted by Johnny Snell, Mr Hinge's secretary, and invited to talk about my career to Mr Hinge at his offices above the Tatler Cinema in Northumberland Street, Newcastle. He must have been keen to have me as he agreed to pay me a £5 per week retainer in the event of no work. But there was plenty of work at £12 per week and for the next few years I toured all around the North-East theatres with artists like Jimmy Gay and Jack Mayo. Some of my longest runs were in touring revues called 'Join The Party' and 'Get Cracking'.

Around 1949/50, I started to hear about a Geordie comedian called Bobby Thompson who was enjoying great success at the Grand Theatre, Byker. Eventually, when I wasn't working away, I caught his act at the Grand and took to his little character straightaway. I think that Bobby signed up with E.J. Hinge in 1951 and Andrew Thewlis, who was one of Hinge's touring managers, took him down to Peterborough to play Buttons in the pantomime 'Cinderella'. However, because of his dialect, it was not very successful and after that Bobby stayed local. Shortly afterwards, we met formally for the first time when Bobby, who was having a meal with E.J. Hinge in his Tatler cafe, came over to my table to introduce himself. We kept in touch after that, but didn't see very much of each other as we were both busy touring. Around 1953, I was over in Austria entertaining US troops when I became ill with yellow jaundice. As the contract was of the 'No-Show-No-Pay' variety, I had no choice but to go home. After recovery, I started to work more in clubs as theatre work was drying up.

Our friendship developed when he moved to Monkseaton - not far from my Shiremoor home. This move was after his Tyne Tees episode and Bobby was finding it difficult to get work, even in the clubs. If I had a spare hour or so, I would drop in to see Bobby, Phyllis and the boys. As you know, they never locked the door and I just used to walk straight into their home. At that time, I worked full time as a representative for Rediffusion and, if I had been out into the country, I'd drop in to see Bobby and give him a chicken and some fresh eggs - as he was a pal. We got on very well. We were both showbusiness pros and both enjoyed a drink and a bet. He was a likeable rogue and very good company, even when he was telling you a tale. I'd come away and analyse the conversation. Then, the penny would drop and I realised that he'd been having me on and laughing up his sleeve. I never saw him rehearse, ever, but he would be rehearsing the whole time he was talking to you, either in his home or a pub. We used to meet twice a week for a pint and a game of dominoes in his local pub, The Ship, which he also used as his office. He was so comfortable there that he travelled back and forth in his slippers. I never lent him money because I knew he would never pay it back. We often got each other bookings through the years and I used to get him spots at my regular venue, the Station Hotel at Whitley Bay, for thirty shillings. That was reasonable money then, as rent would only be about ten shillings and sixpence. Phyllis would nearly always come with him to the Station. I remember her as a big lady who smoked a lot. She could be very jovial and at other times looked non-plussed. She had been through some bad times with him and if they had £3 between them they felt like millionaires. As soon as he moved to go out anywhere, she was there with him. As a couple, they were evenly matched, six and two threes. Phyllis did live to see the good times again, but you are talking about the £15 fee mark in the mid-Sixties and not the £200-£300 a time that he earned later at his peak.

The night that Phyllis was taken to Preston hospital, I got a call from Bobby and went through to take him and the boys to see her. The four of us were there when she died. Bobby was devastated. He had two bookings for the following night, at the Ritz Bingo, North Shields and New Hartley Workingmen's Club. At his request, I fulfilled both bookings for him. On the following Tuesday, after the funeral, he was telling us that he could never face an audience again. Paddy Fox, his wife Rosie, myself and one or two other pals took him out for the night to the Robin Hood pub at Murton Village, near Monkseaton. I got up on stage and then made Bobby get up to say a few words. He managed to speak to the audience and realised that he could get on entertaining, in spite of Phyllis's death.

I remember the time that he took ill a year or so after Phyllis died, when Lottie Tate was his housekeeper. We were returning from a booking in my car (I'm sure that he gave me and others bookings with him because we had cars to transport him around) when he started to vomit blood. I drove him straight to hospital. They let him out after tests, but he was soon back in again and it took three months for him to get better. I used to visit him in the Hadrian Hospital, Wallsend. One day, he said to me in a dead serious tone: 'Pat, the vicar's been in and he's been giving me books and oranges. He's a canny lad, a lovely lad.'
I said: 'Well that's very nice of him.'
When I went in again, he said: 'Pat, that vicar's been in again, but I don't know what to say to him.'
I took no notice and didn't realise that he was trying to pick my brains for what to say. On my next visit something was still bothering him. 'That vicar is lovely, really kind, but I don't know what to say to him, he's not one of us.'
'Ah,' I said, 'now I know what you mean.'
I thought Bobby meant that the vicar fancied him, but Bobby said: 'Why na, no, man, nothing like that. He's so kind I don't like to tell him. He's Church of England and I'm a Catholic, and if I tell him he'll stop giving me the books and oranges.'

People rightly paid tribute to Brian Shelley for re-launching him, but to me the person who really put him on the road to success was his housekeeper, Lottie Tate. She was a lovely woman who was devoted to Bobby and his lads, but more importantly she dressed him like a new pin, and this was an unusual departure for Bobby. All of his clothes were kept immaculate and she made sure that he didn't go out looking untidy. This gave Bobby a new image and a feeling of confidence which, added to Shelley's guidance and his own reliability since giving up drink, accelerated his climb.

Our meetings were not as regular when his career really took off in the Seventies, as he really was kept very busy, but when we did get together he was the same Bobby Thompson. He used to drop in to see me at the Station Hotel and always retained a soft spot for the Robin Hood pub. At the height of his fame, I have seen him do his act there for free, just because he wanted to.

As a fellow entertainer, I have tried to analyse the undoubted success of his act (which had little variation) and sometimes wondered if I was jealous of it. When you can walk out in front of an audience and have them laughing before you've opened your mouth, then you've really got something. Certainly, no matter how many times I heard his material, he could always make me laugh.

The last time I saw him was a couple of months before he died. There was a story going round that Michael had taken a knife to him over a money dispute. He was very upset when we talked. I don't like to think of him in those latter days, it is too sad. I think only of the good chats and times we had and how lucky we both were to be in showbusiness in the Forties and Fifties - it was a wonderful life. For me, it would have been a tragedy not to have known Bobby Thompson. Although he was in showbusiness, he didn't have a celebrity's life. He lived the life of an ordinary workingman. Above all, he was, what the world these days is sadly short of, a real character. Perhaps, being Irish, I appreciated that more than anything else.

MRS LILY COATES

The Thompson family came into my life around 1950/1 when I lived in Barley Mow and used to see Phyllis Thompson pushing her two small sons in a big green pram past my mother's (Chrissie Elliott) door. They had moved in to live with Ernie Green and his wife. I offered to take the bairns up to the shop and back and that is how I got to know her and Bobby.

Bobby was just doing local turns at that time and was well liked in the neighbourhood as a character and a comedian. He got a start, either through the dole office or my brother Ralph, with the builder Higgs and Hill on the site of Henly's Cables (now AEI) at Barley Mow which was practically opposite my mother's home. My husband, Ivan, was his foreman. His job was to act as a can-boy for the building workers - make their tea and general running around. He turned up for work wearing silver lame trousers. By all accounts he was a good worker who turned up on time.

At the beginning of every week Bobby would collect the money from the men to buy the tea and sugar. Each week he would take a bit out of the packets and give it to my mother for safekeeping until he could pick up his packets to take home when work had finished. My mother was always baking stotty cakes and corned beef and potato pies and used to put them on her front windowsill to cool. She always knew when Bobby had been over as there was always one item missing. Nobody ever thought of him as a thief. Things were just there and he helped himself and my mother was only too pleased to give her baking away to anyone who asked. Often, Phyllis used to say that they had enjoyed a 'nice bit of pie for tea'. We all smiled but never said anything to her.

Phyllis and I used to go to the Barley Mow Dog Track at Pelaw Grange. She was a big woman who often wore a fur coat and white sand-shoes. A little rough but with good points is how I would describe her. She had a nice cheery personality and was always smiling. They didn't have very much but they were both good parents and really loved their boys.

Phyllis never bared her soul to anyone - if she had any worries or secrets she kept them to herself. As far as his career was concerned, she was right behind him and believed that he had something special.

It was evident that they were a close couple by their eye contact in company, but they did bicker a lot - sometimes seriously, sometimes good naturedly. He was nagged but not without cause on Phyllis's part. Bobby was a bit of a lad and used to chat up the women by going over to their company, having a few words and buying them a drink. Phyllis used to pay him back by getting a half of beer (they always drank half pints) in for herself when he was in other company. When he returned to Phyllis's table and saw that she hadn't got him a drink, he would lose his temper. Things between them would simmer down and he would make it up by getting up and buying them both a drink.

I remained friends with the Thompsons but lost social contact as I had my own small family and then moved to Lumley. Shortly after my move there, they shifted to Lumley, where they had been given a council house of their own in Lowfield Crescent, and the friendship resumed. One day Bobby came into the Dog and Gun pub at Lumley, where I was working as a barmaid, and asked me to cash a cheque for £7 10s. I think that it was the first cheque he had ever received and he wasn't very pleased to be paid in this way. In order that I could put it through the till properly, he asked me to take orders for the few people who were in the bar. One lady tried to order a gin and orange, but he said: 'To hell with that game, give her a half of beer.'

Bobby and Phyllis gave a party at their Lumley home and I did the catering and waiting-on for them. The friendship was interrupted when I moved back to Barley Mow and the Thompsons moved to Sunderland. However, it resumed some years later when the Thompsons moved back in with the Greens at Barley Mow following the bad time with Bobby's Tyne Tees Television shows in 1959. I went to see Bobby do his act at the Barley Mow pub and got back in with Phyllis by sitting with them.

My sister and I went to see him in the Fifties at Newcastle Empire

Theatre. He saw me in the audience, made me stand up and told everyone that I had got my fur coat out of a catalogue!

I lost real touch when the Thompsons moved to Whitley Bay and was very sad to hear of Phyllis's death in the Sixties. I had to work that day and couldn't attend her funeral.

In the 1970's I met up with Bobby again and his son, Michael, when they used to visit George Gill's Azure Blue pub in Gateshead. Bobby's pal, Paddy Fox, used to come in with them. At that time, I was working as manageress of the Black Bull in Gateshead and after closing up I would go down to the Azure Blue. He always remembered me as Johnny Elliott's daughter and signed his record cover and a photograph to me. Bobby and George Gill, who was a real gentleman, were good friends and enjoyed each other's company. On one occasion, in the Azure Blue, a gay made advances to Michael Thompson and Bobby lost his temper, but George sorted it out. Bobby was drinking bitter lemons then, but was still cheerful and friendly - he was always great to know.

'Come on, Topsy, aa'll get you a tin of Whiskas.'
Aa says: 'Cut some off ya mother's chin.'

MICHAEL THOMPSON - 'WOR TADGER'

I was born on November 15, 1948. I have little recall of very early childhood days, but from what people have told me, dad used to push me all over in the pram. When he wanted a drink, he used to take the pram into the pub, park it in a corner, and give me something to play with. I can just remember a pub in Chester-le-Street, called The Queens, and we were always told to call the couple who ran it Mammy and Daddy Rose. My first clear memory is from when I was three or four years old and we lived in Barley Mow, Birtley, Co. Durham. We lived with some friends called Green and called them Mammy and Daddy Green. We first knew Mrs Green as a bit of a tartar - sort of not unpleasant, but didn't smile a lot. My mother got talking to her at a bus stop one day and became friendly with her. Soon, we became their greatest friends and moved in with them for three years. Four of us (my mam, dad, younger brother Keith and I) shared one bedroom and the Greens had the other bedroom. My dad got a job on a building site as a labourer and the firm, I think, was Hill and Higgs. He was a jack of all trades - tea boy, digger etc. The day he started, he went to work in a pair of brand new silver-grey pants and, of course, he had the mickey taken out of him all the time. But he proved he could work - he was a damn good worker.

Eventually, jobs in workingmen's clubs started to come in, followed by radio and theatre work - very little money, enough to pay board and rent. That was in the early Fifties, 1953 or 54. By that time, we had a council house in Lowfield, Lumley, Co. Durham - returning to Barley Mow every other day to see the Greens. Dad's show at the Grand Theatre, Byker, ran for fourteen months, but it didn't pay much. My mother used to sit in the gallery, in her big fur coat, watching the show, walking down the aisle, sitting in the front. Keith and I used to go occasionally.

One of my earliest recollections of my father was when I was very young and he was in pantomime, 'Little Bo Peep', at the Grand Theatre, Byker, Newcastle. There were two sheep in the show, called Custard and Jelly, and they stayed in our back garden in Lumley. A van used to pick them up everyday and bring them back each night after the shows. He did this for Keith and myself so that we had the pleasure of looking after them. We also had a horse for three or four months and used to ride it through the village. I think it came from a 'Cinderella' pantomime and used to pull the coach, but I'm not certain. Anyway, we ended up with the horse, but eventually we got rid of it as it was too big to cope with. I can't really remember the Grand Theatre itself, although I pass the site of it sometimes.

I remember old Mr Hinge who owned the theatre and some cinemas as well. He was a right tartar. He had a secretary, called Miss Yeats, who ran the show and was hated by one and all. She used to supervise the Tapper Girls, who were the dancers in the 'Merry Magpies' show, and I think my dad took a liking to one or two of those. He got on well with all of them. They stuck together and were a successful team for years.

With all the show-girls around, my mother was possibly jealous at first. However, I think she got used to it and after four or five years had a couldn't-care-less attitude. Sometimes, he used to go away for a couple of days - no-one knew where he was - but he always came back. He used to drink like a fish. I remember once he was at Redcar, at the old Odeon Cinema, and we were staying in a boarding house. He was so drunk, we could hardly wake him up to go for the night-time performance. Of course, I was frightened - I wasn't very old. Keith didn't know much about it. Eventually, we got him sobered up and he went on.

Drink was definitely his big problem in the early days. My mother also liked a drink, but never got sozzled. As a couple they got on very well. They used to have their arguments and rows and my dad used to go for the clock and smash it off the wall. He bought her a new one and she threw it down the stairs and smashed it to bits. That was it, he never touched a clock again.

As my father's career improved, we left the council house in Lumley and got a house in Ewesley Road, Sunderland. It was built by a relative of Yuill (the builder) for Freddy Rout, my dad's manager. This was around 1959, about the time of the Tyne Tees flop. Dad was buying this Sunderland house, but had to let it go later that year.

In the Fifties, we had a gypsy existence, with my dad working theatres and travelling around in a caravan, but it didn't seem to bother us or affect our education in any way. There was never any difficulty getting into a local school and we knew that we weren't stuck there if we didn't like it. We met a number of celebrities - my dad was once on a variety bill with Arthur Lucan, who was Old Mother Riley. When he used to play Sunderland Empire, we lived in a caravan next door to the theatre and I remember people like Craig Douglas coming to visit us. I would not wish to have changed my childhood or had different parents.

Dad had a good friend at this time, called Mousey Hartley, who came from Chester-le-Street, and he used to travel all over with us. If my dad had a job away, we all went with him - including Mousey. Mousey had his own little bed-sit in the caravan. He was a stocky little man, balding with glasses, who played the spoons and would keep us kids occupied for hours. I don't think there was anything between my mother and Mousey. My mother once told me that she wasn't interested in other men - she said that my dad was enough.

My mother was very protective and affectionate. I wasn't close to my father until after my mother died. He used to 'play away' a lot. I remember once, we were at a boarding house in Sunderland and he was between jobs. He had finished a pantomime season at Sunderland Empire ('Mother Goose', 1961/2, with Craig Douglas and Nat Jackley) which earned him £50 a week and, as usual, we had been living in the caravan. The boarding house provided meals and we were all living in one room. One day, my father went through to Washington and my mother only had coppers left in her purse. He promised to be back the same night, but didn't return. The next morning, she got us on the bus to go into Sunderland and had fourpence left after paying our fares. She saw my dad standing at a bus stop. We got off the bus, but I won't tell you what she called him. He didn't tip up all his money to her - he kept money for himself. When he had cash, we never went short of a thing. He had done a job the night before and stayed at this lady's house. We learnt all this later - my mother had her contacts and found out about it. If his behaviour hurt her, then she never showed it to us. In a row, my mother could certainly hold her own.

We were never badly treated or smacked, and he was even-handed with Keith and myself as children. He talked about his own childhood, losing his parents at an early age, no shoes and going barefoot to school. He spoke of men putting their suits in pawn on a Monday and getting them back on a Friday. He came from a very big family. He was close to Uncle Jack and Auntie Rosina and saw them often. We laughed when he told us that he would dodge his work down the pit, if he could, with a little help from his friend from those days, Norman Finnegan, who died a few years ago. He used to hide behind Norman Finnegan's couch and Rosina used to come in and ask if Norman had seen 'our Bobby'. Norman would say: 'Eeh, no,' and Rosina would say what she was going to do with him when she found him. All this time, my father would be laughing behind the couch, waiting for her to go. Once Rosina had gone, Norman and my dad used to head for a dance in Houghton-le-Spring or Penshaw. Dad wasn't badly treated as a child. The past didn't make him tight-fisted with us and, as kids, he spoiled us as long as he had the money. I got a brand new three-wheeler tricycle with a little red boot on the back. We were playing in the woods near Great Lumley - I was about five or six. I saw this other boy playing with a top and whip and we traded. When I got home, mother said: 'Where's your bike?' I said: 'I've swapped it for this top and whip.' She was out of the house like a shot, straight down to the other lad's home to see his mother - they were both in hysterics. Mam got the tricycle back straightaway.

Once, during his years with the 'Merry Magpies', we were staying in a caravan at Workington - funny little thing it was, but it did us. On a whim, my mother sent us to school dressed in kilts for a week - funnily enough, no-one took the mickey. I think they put it down to us being strangers. I remember we had some friends at Workington and moved out of the caravan and in with them. Dad's roving eye with the ladies started again. I don't know how he did it - he was like a magnet. Maybe it was because he was the star of the show - and around this time (1957) he would still be a relatively young man - but he certainly had a way with the women. My mother knew what was going on and must have given him hell. In fact, I know she did. Let's face it, anyone can do anything behind some one's back. There were ways and means. The shows were twice nightly and he would go out drinking in the afternoons. What he did through the day, after he left the pub, I don't know.

My mother used to drink and play dominoes. They both enjoyed the game and my father was a wizard. At the finish, she just drank orange juice and played dominoes. People used to say that he knew where every domino on the board was. In the end, no one would play him - he cleaned up. He and a friend, Pat Healy, went to a club in Shiremoor and were nearly barred because they won £28 - a lot of money when you play for five and ten pences. The members thought there was something fishy going on, but he was a fantastic player.

I've seen him play and studied his game. He'd say to a player: 'You won't play that,' and he knew what the domino was - it was the four-six. The bloke would turn over the domino and it was the four-six. How he knew, I don't know. They would take him on, thinking this little bloke can't beat me - even the best players in the pub. Yet, he never got into fights - he was too careful and discreet. My father wasn't a man who made many friends or enemies. No one actually tried to damage him as far as I know. Certainly, had he been in trouble like that, he had some very hard people to stick up for him.

He once told my mother that he was going to stay with a woman, called Gwen, who was in a show they were doing as the 'Merry Magpies' at Sunderland Empire. I went with him. Dad had primed me as to what I should say on our return, but when mam asked me where I'd been, I said exactly the opposite. It turned out that we'd been to see a dancer with whom he was having an affair. I remember her walking down the stairs at Sunderland Empire and saying to my mother: 'I'm going to have your husband.' My mother turned round and said: 'You take him, you're welcome, but you won't have him long.'

He never left my mother, but continued to have the affair until it petered out. Dad got away with things that a lot of other people wouldn't. He used to charm people - he did. I have seen him do it. Women used to hunt him. I've seen women go into his dressing-room, just after he came off stage. I saw Cissie go in one night and almost pull a woman out. 'That's my husband,' she said.

Drink caused a lot of his illness. He was twice in hospital with TB - once for four months, and once for three months in the Hadrian Hospital. The first time was when we lived in Lumley, around 1953. My dad was working away, it might have been Leeds, and I recall my mam getting a phone call. I remember the police coming to our door and me getting told off, by my mother, for calling them the 'polis'. 'It's the police, not the polis,' she told me. Deprivation in childhood and smoking were probably the main causes, although he told me that he didn't inhale from cigarettes - which was hard to credit for someone who smoked so many a day. But I have no reason not to believe him. He was always bad with his chest and had chronic bronchitis.

In 1959, Tyne Tees Television hadn't been going long and they were using a lot of network programmes, as they had very few of their own. My dad's show was meant to be a big success for the company, and for most of the four month run they put it out at 9.30pm, after 'Wagon Train'. The first three shows were quite good (my parents wrote the scripts for the first two) but after that it deteriorated rapidly. The producer was Philip Jones, and when he did an interview for my dad's Channel 4 programme, he said that Bobby Thompson had simply not been right for television at that time. Whereas Morecambe and Wise had made the transfer from stage to TV brilliantly, my dad hadn't. He didn't put the blame on Tyne Tees shows at all - just that my dad wasn't ready. On radio, Richard Kelly was there to guide him, support him and tell him what to do. He was also a disciplinarian and I think my dad needed that strength behind him.

In the 1958/59 pantomime season, he appeared in 'Aladdin', with Eve Boswell, at the Empire Theatre, Newcastle. It was a very big success and he was working for Tom Arnold. On the strength of that, they almost immediately booked him again to do 'Cinderella' the following year at the same theatre. As a result of the Tyne Tees shows, my dad found himself second on the 1959/60 pantomime bill to a double act - one of them used to work with Jimmy Clitheroe, but I can't recall their names. However, they pulled out three weeks before the show and my dad became top of the bill. They couldn't have cancelled my dad, even if they'd wanted to, as he had a signed contract. That panto, which had Danny La Rue as one of the Ugly Sisters, wasn't as successful as the 'Aladdin' run in the previous season and it was after this that things started to go downhill for him.

After the Tyne Tees flop, in 1959, we went back to Barley Mow to stay with the Greens and then got the place in Whitley Bay. My dad was down for about five years after Tyne Tees and had to do 'Go-As-You-Pleases'. I remember having to take pop bottles back to shops, so that he could use the deposits towards his bus fares. When he had to do these club talent shows to support his family, he felt humiliated if he didn't win. He would travel to Morpeth from Whitley Bay, by bus, just for a spot or a 'Go-As-You-Please' competition. There were no taxis back for him, but he went out night after night to do the best that he could. If you were lucky and won a 'Go-As-You-Please', you got four or five quid. He used to do four or five of these a week at different clubs. He used to win most of them, but even when he was placed second he thought the judges had rigged it. He always seemed to come back with something - even if it was just a couple of quid. A few quid in those days would get you through the day. If he won the round, he would go into the final and he usually won those. People were amazingly generous - ordinary people in the clubs used to buy him drinks because they knew he was down on his luck. His favourite medium was always workingmen's clubs, even though he had been more in the theatre during the Fifties. He liked the atmosphere in the clubs and he liked the people. Whatever money he earned from those nights was given to family needs.

It was a great time of stress for my mother, particularly when my dad went into hospital. She didn't realise that she could get money from the Social Security. The manager of the Whitley Bay Social Security office, who was in the next bed to my father at the Hadrian Hospital in 1966, told dad how my mother could make a claim. Eventually, we got a book. Social Security paid the rent and we had money for food while he was in hospital. My mother couldn't work, she'd suffered a heart attack in her forties when my dad was playing at Rotherham - around 1955. She was very poorly. My dad was very good to her and treated her well.

Billy Botto put my dad back on his feet. He knew dad from clubs and theatres and stuck by him. As soon as dad came out of hospital, he gave him a week's booking, for £100, at Billy Botto's Club in Shields Road West, Byker, Newcastle. After that, he had regular bookings there every few months and the money got bigger. People, who dad had treated well when he was in the money, didn't want to know him when he was down and my dad never forgot that.

He never had any expectations of me personally. My leaving the Civil Service, in 1971, didn't please him, and when I joined Ladbroke's he was against that. Eventually, I won him round and he was quite pleased as they were a good firm to work for. His own lack of education never bothered him, but he thought that schooling was important for us. He took me to school a few times. When we moved to Whitley Bay, he accompanied me to the new school. I was eleven at the time and didn't need anyone taking me, but it was my first day. He never felt that he was better than anyone else, nor did he feel inferior to anyone - either educationally or career-wise. He was pleased how his career had developed, having been part of show business since he was fourteen. He didn't pay much attention to home life, and was content as long as he got his meals and could go out for a drink. If I had a problem, I'd go to my mother rather than my father. He would help you, if you went to him, but it was no use going to him with your homework.

My mother was brainy. My dad was highly intelligent with a good memory, but wasn't academically inclined. The bulk of his shows were

45

not scripted as such. His routines were repetitive, but his memory had to be spot-on to do acts of up to 45 minutes, without making a single mistake. He used the same amazing memory to great effect when playing dominoes. I've seen his act dozens of times in the clubs - some of his jokes made me laugh, but some didn't. Keith would be sitting there roaring with laughter and I'd be po-faced. Yet, some of his jokes, and I think it was the way he told them, made me keel over with laughter.

We nearly always had a dog - he loved them. One of the dogs, Peter, lasted fifteen years until he was knocked down. Peter went missing once for three months and a friend, Jeff Holland, came down the street with it one day saying: 'I've found your dog.' My father was convinced that he had pinched it in the first place, but he hadn't, it was just my dad's suspicious mind. Jeff was driving in Seaton Delaval one day and saw a bloke with Peter on a leash. Jeff opened the door, shouted 'Peter' - the dog broke free, jumped into the car, and Jeff drove off leaving the bloke standing.

His unreliability for bookings surfaced around 1961, after his fall. Before that, for example in the 'Merry Magpie' days, I don't believe he had a problem. He would agree to play one club for £6 and then turn up for another who had come along later and offered £8. Sometimes, he didn't turn up at all. His main drink, in those days, was beer, but I believe he liked the odd whisky. I've seen him sink some booze without turning a hair.

I remember the night my mother died. She had suffered a heart attack and was downstairs, in bed, for three weeks at Princes Gardens. Then she took a stroke and was admitted to hospital. Two weeks later, I phoned the hospital from work one day and they told me that she was deteriorating. When I got home, dad was getting ready to go to the hospital and I said: 'We'd better go now.' Pat Healy drove us there and we were with her at the end.

Keith was sixteen at the time and I was working in the Civil Service at Longbenton. Dad used to look after us and cook the meals. Previously, I never saw him do any work in the house at all. He coped magnificently, did the housework, hoovered, did the beds and had a meal ready for us at night. I used to go to the launderette to get our washing done, but he did everything else. He took to it like a duck to water - he simply didn't want to see us go down. He took my mother's death very badly. We needed a housekeeper and the landlady of The Ship, Monkseaton, where I used to drink, said that she would deal with it. She did the interviews and picked Lottie Tate, who stayed with us until she died - about thirteen years. She was a widow from Wallsend. My dad took to Lottie straightaway, but I didn't take to her until she'd been with us for about a year. After a time, they lived as man and wife. When he told me that he was thinking about getting married again, I made it clear that I was not very happy. I think he had second thoughts and then decided he didn't want to marry her. Lottie wanted to marry my dad at first, and really thought a lot of him - she must have done to stick it for thirteen years. She always had a single room for the whole time, but they were a couple.

Dad was very popular with the ladies and I knew about one or two of his liaisons, but I just kept my mouth shut. It was none of my business what he got up to. One of the ladies, Mabel, was canny, she was well off - had a business somewhere in the Chester-le-Street area - and wanted to marry him. She was really nice and I think that my dad thought an awful lot of her at the time. This was after my mother died. I used to like her and telephoned her a lot, even when I worked away in London. If he had married her, I would have been happy. She was either divorced or widowed - I think she was widowed. Unfortunately, she and my dad drifted apart. Keith and I were really sorry, as we both thought a lot of her - she was a proper lady. She used to visit us in Monkseaton and we used to go to her home and her son's home. Lottie Tate was around at the time, but I think she was told, in a roundabout way, that it was none of her business as she was only the housekeeper. I think, at that stage, things had come to a head between Lottie and my father and they realised that they were never going to marry.

Lottie had a wicked temper - I've never known a woman with a bad temper like her, but she had a heart of gold. She knew dad was philandering, but really did look after him. Every shirt he wore was washed by hand - she wouldn't use a washing machine for his shirts - they were all done in cold water. He was turned out like a king, even though they had their wild rows. Lottie was a good cook and dad liked good plain food, particularly meat puddings. He enjoyed an occasional steak and his favourite dessert was apple pie and custard. Breakfast was always half a grapefruit, toast and several cups of strong treacly tea. He usually had a sandwich at lunch-time and a good meal about four o'clock. He always had something to eat late at night.

My dad never played around near to home. I got involved one night when he went out with a friend's mother. I had to tell a lie. We were supposed to be going to the dogs, and we did go, but we didn't tell Lottie that we were picking up dad's lady friend. The three of us went to the dogs, but I left and they went somewhere else. When I went home, I just told Lottie that my dad had gone on to the casino in Newcastle, where he was a member. Nevertheless, she found out about it - eventually. Of course, there was a right royal row, but my dad came out on top again - he did just what he liked.

Paddy Fox was my dad's best friend. Paddy and Rosie used to come through to our Monkseaton home, before he married Cissie, and stay for three or four days. We used to have some great times when Lottie was alive. We used to go on holiday together and take Paddy and Rosie to Blackpool with us. He used to pack my dad's costume-case for him, unpack it in the club at the other end, and dress him during the show. He was tickled pink to do it and dead proud. My dad often used to give Paddy money. Every time Paddy came through to Monkseaton, he'd get a back-hander and a load of cigarettes. Paddy had been pretty poorly and hadn't worked for some years. He and my dad were always at the betting shops - my dad was a gambling fanatic. He didn't gamble as much when he was drinking, apart from the dominoes. When he stopped drinking, I think he needed another interest.

The Blackpool holiday for my dad, Lottie, Paddy and Rosie was always two weeks in a small bed-and-breakfast house, and out every night to a workingmen's club. Invariably, straight after breakfast, they would go to a café for another cup of tea. I would go out with them, but I didn't stay in the same place as them, because I didn't want them to know what time I came in or vice-versa. I just wanted to be on my own. I used to go out with them in the morning to the café for a cup of tea, then depart. Although, by this time, my dad didn't drink alcohol, I'd go into a pub or club with him and Paddy and have a few pints. Paddy drank, but not very much.

Lottie and Rosie would go for a look round the shops. They'd all meet at lunch-time for a snack, a sandwich or something, nothing heavy. In the afternoons, Lottie and Rosie would go to the Coral Bingo, Sundays included. Dad and Paddy were supposedly at the betting shop all day. Now, I know my dad liked the betting shops, but there's no way that they'd be in the betting shop from one o'clock to five o'clock. I honestly don't know what they did every afternoon for a fortnight, but they certainly weren't in the betting shop. Women were fascinated by my dad - all types went for him. Paddy was probably there as a minder or go-between.

They would be booked in for the evening meal and afterwards all four would go to a workingmen's club. On the way back to the digs, they'd eat fish and chips in the street. They'd sit up until 3.00am, the organist would play and my dad would be entertaining the other guests. The place would be packed - he couldn't resist it. If someone said: 'Will you do a turn for us tonight?' he would have said: 'I'm doing no turn.' Left alone, he would entertain of his own accord.

Dad stopped drinking when Lottie lived with us. I remember the night it happened. He had been to Doreen's, Lottie's sister, and he was carried in absolutely legless. Lottie said to him: 'Look, these lads have lost their mother and, the way you're going, they'll have no father.' It must have hit him hard, because he never had another drink from that day. Of course, when he gave up the drink, his reliability increased, the bookings came pouring in and the money went up and up. Lottie and dad used to fight a lot, but it was never carried over to the next day. He'd get up the next morning, have a cup of tea and ask her if she was all right. Even when they fought, she would still go to the club with him and sit laughing at his jokes. For all they lived as a couple, he paid her for being a housekeeper throughout those thirteen years. When he had his first record success, he gave her quite a bit of money. She had her time off - most afternoons and evenings for the bingo. He didn't mind as long as she did everything she was supposed to do - which she always did. With my mother, he was always very affectionate and buying things for her, but with Lottie not quite so much - perhaps for fear of offending Keith and myself. Dad thought the world of Lottie and was badly cut up when she died. For all her bad temper, she was fun and very generous.

After Lottie, we got a young housekeeper, Binnie, who didn't live in. My dad had met her in The Little Waster pub, in Wallsend, and they got talking - that's how she offered to work for him. She came in every day to do the washing and cook the meals.

Mary Douglas, Lottie's sister, who my dad became engaged to a few years after Lottie died, was nearly her double. She wore glasses, like Lottie, but wasn't quite as plump. My dad already knew her and, as she was a widow, he started taking her to clubs. When they became formally engaged, I really blew my stack. I didn't particularly like her, but I made it up with my dad and told him that we both had our own lives to live, and it was his happiness that counted in the end. Although Mary never moved in with dad, she would come through to cook lunch on Sunday and visit us through the week. Occasionally, she stayed overnight and my dad had Eddie drive her back and forth. Dad was never inclined to drive and had no interest in cars - other than for convenience and comfort. He was nervous of them because he had gone through the windscreen when he was younger and suffered scarring. At one point, the papers made a lot of him having a chauffeured Rolls Royce, but it was only on hire for a week to get publicity.

The relationship between dad and Mary lasted about a year and broke up one Boxing Day, when she asked my dad to lend her so many thousands of pounds for her son to buy a pub. My dad knew the bloke from the brewery and asked about the pub. He told him, in no uncertain terms, what he thought of the place and why the tenancy was up for sale. As a result, dad wouldn't lend her the money. That was the start and finish of it. Mary had £4,000 belonging to him and he sent his taxi driver, Eddie, to go to the house and collect the money. It was all in cash and apparently he'd given it to her for safe-keeping. Eddie got the money back. Mary liked my dad - most women did - but it just didn't work out.

Binnie was some company, but I think my dad wanted a live-in housekeeper, so we advertised and Cissie Palmer came. My dad kept Binnie on for a while, two days a week, after Cissie arrived, but that arrangement didn't last long.

Cissie came from Stanley. At first, it was on a daily basis, but that only lasted a matter of weeks and then she just moved in. I didn't take to her straightaway, but eventually I quite liked her - until towards the end when we fell out. I don't think there was any deep affection on my dad's side. She would sit and sign a pile of his photos on the back - 'Best Wishes, Bobby and Cissie Thompson'. I'm sure she would have loved to get up on the stage with him. They were together for some time before he married her, so he must have held her in some regard. It suited him to have her around. Cissie was keen to be Mrs Bobby Thompson and they married on New Year's Eve, 1982. They had no honeymoon as he was working that night. He continued to go to Blackpool for his holidays, as usual. Once, for a change, they went to Bridlington. We got him talked round to going to the Isle of Man - they even sent off the deposit for the hotel - but he backed out because he didn't want to fly. He never went abroad, or had any wish to do so. The only boat he ever went on was the North Shields Ferry.

Dad staked about £200 a week in bets at Dawson's in Monkseaton and Ladbroke's in Whitley Bay. Although he studied form, my father was a fanatic for dog-racing and used to back practically every combination in the race, so that he had something coming back at the end of the night. I was manager at Ladbroke's betting shop in Whitley Bay, where my dad was a customer, and I didn't know whether to tell him to go to another betting shop or what. Anyway, I was told by my higher-ups that I had to cope with him. Of course, I had to be harder on him than any other customer - just to show he wasn't getting any favours. To have done otherwise would have caused rows in the shop. Naturally, I got it in the neck when I got home. He would start telling jokes in the shop and people couldn't hear the race commentary for laughter. I used to shout: 'Will you shut up, people are trying to listen.' He would make mistakes on his bets and put the wrong times on. I would be shouting: 'You've put the wrong time on this.' One day, I got really shirty with him and said: 'Look, you're not the only bloody customer in this shop, I've got others.' When I got home that night, there was a hell of a row. He had told Lottie and she went down my throat as well. I told them: 'Look, I am the manager of that shop and people have got to see that he is not getting away with anything, or my job won't be worth a penny. As it is, I've got a good relationship with the rest of the customers because he is not getting away with anything.' Later on, he appreciated the point.

Once, I got him £1,100 for a winning bet on a dog-race, when, in actual fact, he should only have had £198. There was only one dog-race meeting on and he put 3.15pm - the time given by the Daily Mirror - when the actual race time was 3.11pm. The dog he backed won at 33-1 and he had a 'yankee' up. I worked the bet out and it came to just over £1,100. I rang head office in London and told them that he had put the wrong time on the bet. They said as far as they were concerned that was treated as a non-runner - he'd put the wrong time down and that was it. I explained that it was in the Daily Mirror and they said 'tough'. My district manager was in the shop when dad came up. We worked it out and it came to £198 under the Head Office orders. I told him not to take the money, but to write in or, better still, send a telegram. He sent a telegram that night and I dictated what he had to say. I got a phone call the next night from the district manager saying: 'Pay the bet in full.' He gave me £100 for helping him.

My firm asked me whether I would have done the same for any other customer. I said: 'Oh, yes, that's my job, I'm the manager of the shop

52

and I've got to see fair play done.' I knew it was fair - I'd looked in the Daily Mirror and they had misprinted the time. If I thought he'd been in the wrong, he would have only got £198. Anyway, they paid him out in full. They offered him a cheque, but he said he wanted cash. I was quite happy with the £100 he gave me, and it was peace at home. Had he not thought he was entitled to the full pay-out, then he would never have pushed the matter - he only wanted what was properly his. It was appreciated by my dad that I would have done the same for any other customer.

He started going to the Casino Royale, Newcastle, in 1978 because I became a member. I used to go only once every couple of months because it's an expensive hobby. He came with me one night and I signed him in, then he joined himself. He used to lose hand over fist, but sometimes he would win a pile. He never had to pay for a meal and a drink in the casino and I was treated the same. He worked in cash and would spend £150 a night, sometimes up to £300 if he got carried away. If he won, there were chips all over the place. Near the end, I don't think he knew which numbers he was on, except each player had a different colour chip so he knew his colour. Then, he got a system of numbers he was backing, so he knew straightaway when the ball went in whether he had anything coming back to him. If the croupier said: 'Twenty-nine black,' he would say: 'I'm up.' That was it. He worked it out for himself, and knew, to the chip, what he had coming back. I've heard him tell a croupier: 'You're wrong pet, you're wrong.' She would say: 'No, no,' and they'd have to get the inspector over. She had tried to give him a hundred chips too many, but he was honest. At the other end of the stick, he wouldn't let them underpay him either. Paddy used to go with him to the casino and have a meal, but not very often - usually when he was over to see us from his Sunderland home. The casino never had to press my father for money. If he ran out of cash, he simply signed them a blank cheque and it was taken to the bank and cleared the next morning. He had a bank account with Lloyds' at Whitley Bay. Although they liked him at the casino, they would never let him off a debt - as I've heard suggested. Business is business, and they don't write off large amounts. Losing didn't bother him a bit - he took it as part of life. He loved gambling as it relieved the boredom when he wasn't working.

A lot of Chinese people played at the Casino Royale, some were very enthusiastic gamblers. If they tried to push in, my father would push them out of the way and say: 'I was here first, pet, and I'm putting my chips on.' If the croupier was going to spin the ball, he would shout: 'Just a minute, pet, I haven't finished putting my chips on, I can't get in for these people!' She'd have to wait until he got his chips on, then spin the ball. He wasn't rude, but he stuck up for himself - he wouldn't let anyone have one over on him. In fact, he would tear them to pieces with his tongue.

Brian Shelley came to our house sometimes, and I would see him at his office if I popped through to Sunderland with my dad. The relationship with Brian Shelley began to go wrong when Brian kept putting him into clubs in areas that he had just recently done. My father would tell him: 'I've just done a club down the road six weeks ago, you can't put me into this club.' Shelley would say: 'No, No,' and my dad would say: 'Oh, yes, you look, check up.' Sure enough, my dad would be right, he would have done a club ten miles away only six weeks before. Well, people were not going to come and see the same show after only six weeks. He had a route. He did a club maybe once every six or eight months and always tried to avoid running bookings close together. I've no idea why Brian was doing this, and he'll have his own side of the story, but my father was getting fed up and that's why he left Brian and joined the Lewis Vaughan agency. Brian Shelley had a horse, 'Paintbox' or 'Paintwagon' - I don't know whether they were in a shared syndicate, but for about a year my father always insisted on backing it - every time it ran.

Ronnie Vaughan, of the agency, was good to my dad. He used to come through on a Monday morning, have a cup of tea, and give him the week's bookings. Dad's fee was going down quite considerably at this time and he had started to make one or two mistakes in the act, which I put down to his age. He was then in his seventies. At the end, he would be on approximately £175 a night, but he did his two-part act (two lots of twenty minutes) right to the end. He always appreciated his audience - the ordinary people who came to see him - but he couldn't stand crawlers or back-slappers. He knew that these were people who wouldn't give him a second glance if he was on the way down, but wanted to be all over him when he was successful.

Before he started to slide down, about eighteen months before he died, he was earning decent money. He knew he was worth it, so that is what he asked for and got. If a club knew that they could fill their concert room and make profit, then they would pay him the money. Had he not been worth it, then they would not have paid him.

I never knew him to rehearse in the house at all, or practise a punchline. However, when he thought up a new joke, he would tell it to me and ask me what I thought of it. He used to come up with some real funnies. Most of his scripts were his own work and he liked to freshen them up occasionally with topical references like the Red Adair story. He could get away with things, because even if they weren't funny he could make them so. He never used a script writer after radio, and when people sent scripts to him he used to return them - the ones I saw were rubbish, anyway.

He used to ask me for old jokes. I recall one where someone had died and the local butcher said: 'Look, I can't lend you any money for the funeral, but bring him up and I'll put him in the fridge for a fortnight.' It was a real cracking joke and I had to think of these old jokes that he hadn't trotted out for a long time. He used to think them over and then put them back into his act.

I can never recall him writing down any material on paper, his hands or anywhere. His timing was the best you'd ever see. Costume-wise he never contemplated any other than his Little Waster outfit, apart from the uniform for his army sketch. Part of the reason for his gansey was, I'm sure, for the effect afterwards when he wore his suit - the difference would be astounding. The reason for people saying: 'He's so smart,' was not perhaps because he was actually all that smart, but the difference between him in a suit and him in a gansey was so dramatic. On reflection, yes, he was smart, really. Audiences didn't expect to see this raggy little man come out, after a show, looking like something from a shop window. His transformation was hard to miss as he invariably insisted on a table for four, at the front, in every club.

I'm not sure whether or not he wanted to make it nationally. Towards the end of his career, he played to a full house at the Wimbledon Theatre and got a standing ovation. He was on Wogan's show on Monday night, and this was the Sunday evening before and the place was sold out - he was over the moon. Charlie Lee was the agent who put the show on at the Wimbledon Theatre and the same man wanted to put my dad on a London Palladium evening concert. A Palladium appearance would have been a nice highlight, but my father wasn't allowed to choose the supporting acts, so he refused to do it. I was there when he told the agent. My dad had the names of the acts who had been on at Wimbledon with him and, as the show had gone a bomb, he wanted to repeat them again at the Palladium. One of the acts was Jean Bennett, who my father had worked with before at Sunderland - she had a really superb voice. However, Charlie Lee wanted to pick the supporting acts himself and that was the finish. There were a lot of rumours flying around about the Palladium business, that he 'chickened out', but they weren't true. He wasn't bothered in the least about the Palladium dropping through, but it was good publicity.

As far as the 'Wogan' appearance was concerned, my father was terrified. In fact, on the Friday before he was due to go, I thought he was going to back out of it, but he conquered his nerves and saw it through. Cissie went down with him. I think they put him up at a big luxury hotel like the Dorchester or Waldorf - that's where he got the shock of the £4 sandwich. He was relieved that the BBC was footing the bill and they treated him well. My father took to Terry Wogan and called him a proper gentleman. His appearance was due to getting his first album into the national charts and, of course, no one outside of the North really knew who he was. They played up the angle of him outselling the John Travolta 'Grease' album in the North-East and it got a few people interested. The BBC contacted him and eventually asked if he would go on 'Wogan'. He got a £300 fee, first-class rail travel and a couple of nights at a big hotel which was too flash for him, it wasn't his type of place.

He used to worry about his dealings with the tax-man and at one time he was actually making payments of £500 per week. Later on, he wasn't making the money to pay them. At one point, I got things held up for a year when I went to see our local M.P., Neville Trotter. He wrote to the Inland Revenue and my dad got a letter saying that the case was being reviewed. It took another year before they decided to make him bankrupt. Keith went with my dad to the court - I think I was working in London at the time - and he told me later that the whole thing was a farce. The examiner seemed to be a great fan of my father and he appeared to take the rise out of the Inland Revenue prosecutor. When the prosecutor said: 'This is Mr Bobby Thompson,' the examiner said: 'Yes, we know who he is, everyone in the place knows who he is.'
The Inland Revenue advocate asked my father if he gambled much. I believe that they wanted him done for gambling all of his money away.
'Oh, yes,' he said. 'I used to have a bet every day.'
'How much did you gamble each day?' the prosecutor asked him.
'Oh, a few shillings,' he replied.
Well, everybody in the place laughed.

The proceedings were put off for five years and at the end of that time he would have been required to go back for a further examination of his affairs. As it turned out, the Inland Revenue never got a penny. He was pleased about that, but don't get me wrong, he paid his bills. He wouldn't diddle anybody on purpose, but he was rather pleased that he didn't have to pay the Inland Revenue anything. Officialdom he didn't like. As far as I know, his dislike didn't stem from any bad experiences like claiming benefit when he was down. He probably wouldn't have known what he could claim for. As I mentioned earlier, the DHSS were very good to us when my dad went into hospital and when he came out he still continued to get benefit. No, he never had any quarrel with the

DHSS, and that had nothing to do with the fact that I used to work for them! He did have a lot of trouble with his National Insurance contributions. The hassle went on for ages because he was late in paying his stamps, having not stamped his card every week. He let it go and found it hard to catch up. He kept getting letters from them. Eventually, he paid it all up and when he was sixty-five he got his full pension. He only ever owed the Inland Revenue.

Dad had an underfloor safe, as most of his club earnings were paid in cash. He never bothered about burglars and in fact we were only burgled once. I had been out for a drink one evening and had come back at about quarter to eleven. Going into our back living-room, at Princes Gardens, to put the television on, I noticed that there was a drawer open. I thought that it was unusual, but couldn't see anything out of place. Suspicious, I went upstairs and there was a cupboard door open where my dad used to keep a statue of himself. It had been in The Little Waster pub at Wallsend, one of the Noble Organisation houses, and when it closed they gave it to my dad. Well, the burglars must have got the shock of their lives seeing that statue, and fled from the house empty-handed. His gold record, silver record and other stuff had been stacked in the front room, ready to remove on their way out. I just phoned the police and told them that we had been burgled. When they came and looked around, the police showed me the back door which the thieves had half sawn off to get into the house. Nothing had been taken at all. He never got bothered at all in Princes Gardens. Occasionally, kids would come to the door and ask if it was right that Bobby Thompson lived there. My dad would go to the door and talk to them, give them a photograph and they would go away as happy as Larry - he never turned people away.

Dad had little bother with audiences, but when he was drinking that may have been a different story. I remember he did Glasgow Empire Theatre once. The place was notorious and this was a Saturday night. The agency would not let him go on as they knew that the crowd booed everybody, even though my father had gone down very well for the whole week - Monday to Friday. They told him that they were not going to have him humiliated. The place would be full, but they would be throwing bananas, tomatoes, everything.

Politically, he was staunch Labour and entertained several miners' conferences.. particularly when Joe Gormley was the boss, but he respected Neville Trotter, a Tory M.P., for helping him.

Despite his ways, he was a very religious man and did a tremendous amount for charities, The Little Sisters of the Poor being one of his favourites - they possibly helped him out as a kid. Father Cass from St. Edward's, Whitley Bay, used to drop round often and they got on great. My father thought an awful lot of him and he did the Requiem Mass when dad died, as he was born a Roman Catholic. My father didn't go to church, but looked forward to Father Cass calling around for a drink and chat through the day. For his part, Father Cass never badgered my father to attend church, but dad was a Catholic through and through. My mother was a Methodist and we attended Methodist Sunday school, but we were never forced in that direction. We were told that we could choose for ourselves when we were older. My dad believed in God and, from what I could see, had no trouble aligning that belief with the way he conducted his life. I never saw him read the Bible, in fact he didn't read much at all apart from the racing columns of the paper. Overall, he was pleased how life had treated him. He went down in the early Sixties, but he overcame it and got back to the top again and stayed there. All right, for the last eighteen months of his life he wasn't at his best - but he stayed at the top.

He was a very emotional man and I have seen him down and depressed many times, but above all he was a fighter. I got to know when to keep my mouth shut and when to speak. Even after his worst times, following the Tyne Tees fiasco, he was determined not to go under. He drank then, but I never saw him sitting in a drunken state at nights feeling sorry for himself. Instead, he pulled himself together and went out to earn whatever he could.

He never talked about his first wife, Anna Marjoram, or his daughter by that marriage, Beatrice. We never knew the reason for the breakdown of the marriage - except that he said they didn't get along. It could have been because of his womanising, I just don't know. I don't think that he ever made any maintenance payments.

I've heard the rumour about him fathering a child to a show girl around 1955/6, but as yet there is no proof one way or the other. If my mother told someone openly that he was going to be a father, but she wasn't the mother, then she could have been having them on. It sounds like something she could well have come out with.

He was a very good dancer, self taught, and did a shadow-dance behind a screen in theatres. It was fantastic - absolutely brilliant. The whole place was in darkness, apart from the stage and back lighting for the screen where he was dancing. The image would go massive and then very small - you could see his feet moving. The audience used to stand up and yell - it was incredible to watch.

My dad always respected talent - very much so. If he didn't like some act, he would say to me: 'They are rubbish, rubbish.' Other comedians, he would deride to me, Cissie or Keith. He loved a local comedian called Walter Gee. My dad thought that he was fantastic. He had good relationships with some acts and others he just tolerated.

When there was a Laurel and Hardy film on TV, he wouldn't miss it. However, he rarely watched television and when he starred with David Jason he really didn't know who he was. He loved appearing on the David Jason 'Cinderella' pantomime when he got such a high fee for simply doing part of his club act as the midnight cabaret. As you say, the kids got up to get their ices and crisps and the mothers, fathers, grannies and grandads stayed in their seats to laugh at his act.

His jewellery, in my opinion, was a quiet way - not really so quiet - to say to people that he had money. A superb bracelet, a really nice gold watch, two sovereign rings. I can remember the two sovereign rings. I was going down to London, to work for Ladbroke's the next day, and this was a Sunday. Mary Douglas, his fiancée at the time, was sitting with us in the back room and was telling him, as she had for some time, that he didn't suit the rings and she didn't like them on him. Dad just took them off and gave them to me saying: 'You might as well wear them, then.' I went to London with two sovereign rings on the Monday morning. Mary had said that she didn't like them and that was it.

My dad would give me anything, and I lived on and off with him at our Princes Gardens home until he died. After that, I left. People have told me that he used to talk about us and he used to worry about me. Like my father, my life hasn't been straighforward, but always he accepted me for what I was at that time. Drink has been a problem with me for some years, just as it was with him, and I will continue to fight as he did. He was proud of me when I became an Executive Officer in the DHSS, and (eventually) prouder still after I left to join Ladbroke's and became a manager of one of their shops. Once, while working for a betting shop, I was drunk and did a stupid thing. I returned to the shop after Saturday closing and borrowed some money - intending to put it right first thing on the Monday morning. I was so worried by my act that I told the police over the weekend. My dad contacted the book-maker and had the money replaced. I lost the job, but he never criticised me.

He couldn't stand homosexuals. I believe he finished with a theatrical agency when I was a young lad because the partners were thought to be gay. My initials are R.M. and my father's were R.M. Many years ago, when he had big money and I did a lot of banking for him and had his proxy, I drew around £30,000 out of his bank account. Most of it went on drinking in London. When he found out, he just accepted it all because he knew that I was ashamed of having robbed him. On one occasion, I had too much to drink and took a bread knife to him in an argument. I had to go to a psychiatric ward for a short time, but he overlooked my behaviour and still loved me.

My memories of him are good. He was never one to tell you how he felt about you or put his arms around you, but we knew that he loved us. I was born first and I agree with people who say that I was his favourite. Keith has always accepted this fact, without it spoiling our relationship as brothers. Whatever interest he may have lacked, my mother made sure that she made it up with both of their sons. They were a match for each other. My mother could be a worrier, but my father accepted what life gave him, made the best of it, and fought back when he had to. They were very close, and as a child I always felt secure and loved, also different because of who my dad was - I was proud of him and still am.

Her mother was on television - PG Tips.

And ya knaa, the bairns rule ya. If ye've got a laddie fifteen year owld, ye can't de nowt with 'im.
Aa've got a laddie, our Tadger, fifteen year owld, strong as a bull, spittin' on the fire. He's put it out twice.

KEITH THOMPSON

My earliest recollections stem from the time we lived in Barley Mow, with a family called Green, and then in our own council houses at Barley Mow and Great Lumley. I used to feel that it was a very poor existence, but having thought about it, things couldn't have been too bad for us. We were the first ones in the street with a telephone (a pay-phone, mind you) which everybody used to use. It was probably installed because my dad was an entertainer. Michael and I were the first ones in the street to have bikes with blow-up tyres - big white ones, back and front. There was a large back garden at Barley Mow and we had a horse and a sheep at one time.

During my early schooldays, we moved around a great deal - wherever my dad's theatre work was located. I remember, very distantly, places like Workington, Harrogate, Leeds and Doncaster. Sometimes we were in digs, but usually in a caravan parked at the back of the theatre. Dad did 14 weeks at Workington Opera House in 'The Merry Magpies'. The original booking was for two weeks, but there was such a demand for tickets they had to extend the run. 'The Merry Magpies' was a tremendous show. Our caravan accommodation at Workington, and many other places, was shared by a man called Mousey Hartley who was from Chester-le-Street. He was a big fat man - I don't know why they called him Mousey - an absolutely lovely bloke and a great friend to Michael and myself. On reflection, he was a closer friend to my mother than he was to my father, but as to whether there was anything in it, I don't know. On one occasion, around this period, I remember getting on a train with mam, dad, Michael, Mousey Hartley and another man. Dad had friends in Corby, near Carlisle, and this train was from Carlisle to Newcastle and we didn't have enough money to buy everyone a ticket. Anyway, we got on the train and it was in the days when inspectors came round to look at tickets. Two of us - dad and Mousey Hartley - didn't have a ticket - don't ask me how we got through the barriers, because I don't know. The inspector came round and people showed him their tickets. Then, he came to Mousey and dad. 'Hello, Bobby, son,' said the inspector, looking down at him, 'how are you?' 'Eeh, absolutely great,' said dad, 'give us a hand with these and tell us what to play.' I think we were playing seven-card brag and this inspector sat with him while dad played the hand under his instruction. Afterwards, he said: 'I'll see you later,' and he never did ask for the tickets.

In retrospect, this nomadic existence would be normal for many entertainers and their families. As youngsters we were fairly well looked after. My recollection is of my mother buying everything and seeing to our schooling. The education side couldn't have been easy, because of our moving around, but neither Michael nor I missed much school. My great love, as a kid, was bikes and I always got new ones. There was a constant supply of toys and mam always made Christmas special for us.

I can recall dad's drinking binges and thinking that he was quite a violent man. I have a vivid recollection of him kneeling on top of my mother and trying to pull her hair out, while I stood screaming at the top of my voice. He wasn't really a father figure - I can't recall him sticking up for us as kids - but so many people seemed to love him and they knocked on the door and rang the bell at all times. In Leeds, where we stayed for a spell, I recall Billy Bremner and Jack Charlton coming to our place, laughing and carrying on with my dad. He was so sought after, I thought is was the normal thing. There were always people around us, other acts, friends or managers. Oddly enough, for all my dad's family had been poor but very close, we didn't see his relatives at our homes. I remember going to see his brother, Jack, in Fatfield, Co. Durham, when I was about ten. It was the first time I had ever seen him. I remember the hairs standing up on the back of my neck as he came out of the bedroom - he was the double of my dad. I was quite scared because his actions were like my dad's and he sounded like him - it was eerie.

I think that we got evicted (for not paying rent) from the Great Lumley council house and moved back (yet again) to live with the Green family. This would be around the mid-Fifties when my dad was earning good money from the theatres and radio, but failing to hold onto any of it.

As a very young child, I can remember feeling awfully embarrassed because of who my dad was, but after those early years I wasn't affected by my father's name again until my teens. At this age, I can remember being really upset when people, for the wrong reasons, compared me with my dad. For example, if I had done something stupid they would say: 'Oh, you're a waster - just like your dad.' Years later, when I lost a sale in my first job in a tailor's shop - I shouldn't have lost the sale - I remember the manager coming to me and saying: 'I thought it was your dad who was the bloody comedian.' I wasn't offended for myself, but I thought they were being derisory to my dad. However, as an eight or nine year old, all I was interested in was football, and dad would come to see me play on occasions. I passed the eleven-plus at Brown's Buildings School and from there went on to senior school. Even at this age, I hadn't seen the end of living in a caravan. My dad was working on several variety bills at Sunderland Empire with people like Craig Douglas, Ronnie Carroll, Millicent Martin and Hughie Green. I remember sitting in our caravan behind the Empire with Craig Douglas, when his record of "Only Sixteen" topped the charts. My dad made a deal with Hoggett's potato crisps - that he would be supplied with crisps in return for mentioning their product during his turn. Craig Douglas, mam, dad, Michael and I would sit around the caravan eating crisps with paste spread on them. When I think about it, my dad got a lot for nothing. Hughie Green used to have a competition in his act, where people from the audience, who participated in his act, got a box of chocolates or bunch of flowers. Somehow, my dad always seemed to acquire some chocolates or flowers.

Freddy Rout, a builder, booked my dad for some shows in a Workington night club that he owned and later became his manager. Mr Rout gave my dad an absolutely magnificent house at 21, Ewesley Road, Sunderland. Of course, we didn't know that my dad was only renting it from him. When dad's career hit the rocks in 1959, after the Tyne Tees TV shows, Freddy Rout and the house disappeared.

There was bad publicity around this time. Dad was fined £20 for not paying off a clothing debt to Brooks Brothers of Chester-le-Street. He managed to turn that around and put it in his act, so that he turns out to be a bloody hero because he's not paid his bills. If I'd had the common sense then, I would have realised that he was a hero and people weren't actually laughing at him and making fun of him, they were laughing with him.

In 1961, we left Barley Mow and the Greens and for some reason relocated to a guest house in Esplanade, Whitley Bay. We were there for several months and Michael and I got settled into Park View School, Whitley Bay. My mother answered an advertisement in the local paper for a rented house at 20, Princes Gardens, Whitley Bay. I went with my dad to see the house. His hair was dishevelled and he had a checky overcoat on with raglan sleeves - it must have been about 50 years old and made by Burtons. I recall he and I walking up the road to see this woman, who obviously recognised him straightaway. He said that he had come to see her about the house and, without even blinking, this Mrs Gowans said: 'You can have it.' My father was almost skipping on the way back to tell mam. As a family, we were absolutely overjoyed to have a place of our own again. We moved in the following Friday or Saturday and it felt just like Christmas. It was an ordinary three bedroom terrace house, but to us it was magnificent. We had the whole place to ourselves for the first time since Great Lumley. By moving to the coast, we felt that we had moved into the highest echelons of society. I suppose that it was from then on that we had stability, regardless of my dad's career highs and lows. We were to be there for 27 years and it was my dad's home until his death.

My dad was depressed after Tyne Tees and didn't want to work, but I can remember my mother pushing him to enter 'Go As You Pleases'. I can remember him coming back from these competitions and not being placed. For donkeys ages, money was hard to come by, but, on reflection, I realise that my dad used to drink such a lot. My mam and dad used to bet on the horses in an effort to bring some big money in. On one occasion, my mam and dad had £2 between them and they decided to put it on this horse. My mother gave dad the money to go down to the book-makers and place the bet and, while he was out, she

66

watched the race on the television. Anyway, the damn thing won at about 7 or 8-1 and we were absolutely ecstatic. I can remember my dad not coming back home and my mother screaming because she knew he'd spent the money. What she didn't know was that he'd never put the bet on in the first place. When he did come back, there was unholy trouble in the house. I can remember me, as I did all the time, bubbling and whingeing while Michael, my brother, comforted my mother. Those are the sort of things that happened continually.

Although I can't ever recall him rehearsing his act, memories come back of arriving home from school and my dad frantically going through material to remember old jokes, asking us to come up with them, or bouncing jokes off us. I can remember coming up with the joke of the spent rent... (wife) 'We'll have a night out and I'll spend the rent.' (husband) 'Well, she must have been paying double 'cos I spent it last week' - and my dad saying: 'Oh, yes, I remember that one.'

I can remember a fellow coming to the house often, and my dad jealously screaming at my mother that this man was spending too much time at the house and accusing her of something. My mother told him that he was talking baloney. If anything had been going on, my dad had probably brought it on himself as he used to spend every afternoon in The Ship or The Black Horse and leave my mam at home. My mother was a cracking drinker who used to drink bottles of export as if they were going out of fashion - so it wasn't just one of them. There's nothing they liked better than to be with friends and enjoy a drink. I can remember being in a pub in Sunderland called The Feathers. It might have been The Three Feathers. Michael and I were about 10 and 9 years old and expected to do a turn by taking off my dad's act, with the cap on and the comedy clothes, for all these friends and relatives who were around. We thought nothing of it at the time, in fact it was quite fun, but it must have been a bit of a spectacle one way or another.

My father worked in Blackpool, at a night-club called the Lobster Pot, in the early Sixties. The place was run by a man called 'Tiny' Prince who was a well known bass player in the early days of Tyne Tees. We were shown up badly going into digs that Yarker and Thompson, my dad's agents, had organised for us. We went in and saw all the signs: 'NO SMOKING', 'WASH YOUR HANDS BEFORE YOU GO IN' etc. My mother just turned round to my dad and said: 'We're not staying here.' I was nearly wetting myself, I was so embarrassed. My dad was frantic and my brother was panicking. We all walked out and wandered up and down the street, trying to find somewhere else to stay, accompanied by the agents who were trying to placate my dad and keep him happy because he must have been their star of the moment.

My mother, later in life, was a spiritualist and would attend meetings. She believed in the hereafter and was quite God-fearing. Her father had been a Wesleyan lay-preacher. On the other hand, she drank continually, smoked like a trooper and liked the blokes.

We weren't privy to either mam or dad's family background and I'm not sure why. Dad never discussed his first wife or his daughter, Beatrice, from that marriage. We got to know things in fragments from other people. There were no grandparents, they had all died long before we were born.

Unfortunately, my mother didn't live in the Monkseaton house all that long. She died in 1967. It is from this time that my memory becomes much clearer. I can remember vividly, my mother dying in Preston Hospital, North Shields. For some time, she had been absolutely convinced that she had cancer, but actually died of a heart attack. I don't think that it was related to worry over my dad's career in any way. She was a big woman, weight-wise, and had suffered her first heart attack in Rotherham, some years before. We were all devastated and dad was hit pretty bad as, for all their arguments, they were very close partners. Shortly after her death, my dad suffered a long illness with tuberculosis and was a patient in the Hadrian Park Hospital for thirteen weeks. While he was there, charity organisations brought him free pyjamas as he didn't have any. Others brought food to him and all sorts of things. He got over the illness and became stronger still. People were kind to us. Mrs Graham, who had The Ship public house at Monkseaton, organised interviews for a housekeeper on dad's behalf. Eventually, they chose a housekeeper, called Lottie Tate, who came from Wallsend, a very nice woman. As things turned out, she was there for thirteen years. She slept with dad and was everything a wife should be, but she was called a housekeeper. Lottie gave up her own home to come and look after us. At the time, Michael had left home and was working in London as a book-maker.

Real financial comfort came to dad a few years after my mother died, but he had made a lot of money long before that - going back to Sunderland Empire when he could be on £200 a week. His drink bill would be £190 - he'd have a tenner left because he had so many hangers-on. I remember bill-toppers, sitting on the steps of Sunderland Empire, stotting drunk - paid for by dad's money. My mother would criticize him later, but at the time she would be helping with the drink - and drank at least as much as dad.

He was good friends with Jack Haig, who died recently, and they used to drink together at the Egypt Cottage pub on City Road, next to Tyne Tees studios. The television station was then owned by George and Alfred Black. I can remember being left with baby-sitters and screaming my head off, but it wasn't all the time. For some reason, he disliked one of the early sports presenters on Tyne Tees because he felt the man put on an accent. Dad used to go berserk when he came on TV, saying: 'That bugger's got two marbles in his mouth.' He hated pretension and, whatever was right or wrong with dad, you cannot say that he was pretentious, overbearing or looked down upon people.

On the night my mother died, our GP, Dr. Hawthorne, told my dad that if he didn't stop drinking he'd be dead. Contrary to popular belief, he didn't stop at that point, but within a year he stopped completely. It was Lottie who got through to him. She told him that Michael and I had lost a mother and if he continued to drink we would also lose a father. An amazing feat really, he must have had great inner strength. The amounts of beer that he could consume were legendary. Former drinking pals in Barley Mow have told me that he could down twelve bottles of

Newcastle Brown Ale. He used to get legless and then go quietly to sleep. A vivid recollection from his drinking days is of him, standing astride the toilet, urinating for seven or eight minutes at a time. I remember lying in bed listening and thinking: 'This isn't possible.' He was like a watering-can and you have to remember that he was only eight stone in weight.

Dad was a bit of a cowboy when it came to dominoes. He was a brilliant player, although he didn't play in later life. He was barred from The Black Horse, in Monkseaton, because he won too much.

Peculiar things happened. On one occasion, when Michael worked at the Ministry of Social Security at Longbenton, Newcastle, he wanted time off because Redcar Races were on and he'd used up his holidays. Without any difficulty, dad got a sick note, from a doctor he was playing dominoes with in The Ship, for Michael to use.

Lottie was great, and was just like a mother without trying to be one. She really smartened dad up and deserves much credit for the successful image of the 70's and 80's. He was at his funniest when Lottie was alive, especially watching TV. He couldn't hear very well and the TV would be on loud. The titles would have just finished rolling at the beginning of a programme and he would start: 'Who's he?' 'What relation are they?' 'What does she want?' You would get this narration all the way through the programme and I am sure he knew what he was doing. If ever 'Crossroads' was on, we'd be laughing, telling him to shut up. At those times, he was genuinely very funny. We had some hilarious moments in the house when he'd drive people round the bend - Lottie in particular - by not giving an ounce of sense. We used to get Lottie in the back kitchen, my dad used to go mad, get her arms up in the air and tickle her. My dad didn't like any aggravation in the house. If we were fighting, which we invariably did, dad used to get himself really irate. He couldn't stand it. The only noise he liked was his own. He never thumped us - since birth, we've all been bigger than my dad. We were all badly upset when she died and the sad way that it happened. Lottie had wounds on her legs which used to bleed occasionally. She had one wound which bled for several weeks and the doctor said that she had to lie down and rest. When I called at the house one afternoon, she was resting on the couch, as she quite often did, but she was delirious. Obviously, I knew there was something badly wrong with her and called an ambulance, but she was dead before arriving at the hospital.

Dad was very disturbed at losing Lottie. Here was a woman he had no doubt been unfaithful to on numerous occasions, but he had forged a very great bond with her. Their relationship lasted over twelve years. He hated her family, or so I thought at the time, but I subsequently found out that he had been having an affair with one of Lottie's relatives. This shouldn't have surprised me in the slightest because this lady used to go and see my dad on any number of occasions. But he did grieve over Lottie. However, it wasn't too long after that when he put an advert in the paper for a housekeeper and that was when Binnie came along. Then another advert brought Cissie and dad let Binnie go.

Friendship never came easy to my dad. I believe that he had formed friendships when he headed the Merry Magpies troupe in the Fifties, but nothing lasting. People who came on the scene later were more acquaintances than friends. We never knew his pre-showbusiness friends, apart from Norman Finnegan, but we did get a glimpse on one occasion. Going back eight or nine years, we returned to a pub called the Barley Mow, in Barley Mow - where we lived for a number of years. Walking into the bar was like going back to a different era. There were all these old men who were my dad's friends. He used to drink with them when he had nothing - eight or nine bottles of Brown Ale. These people were his mates - they all talked to him and called him 'Bobby', but they weren't overawed by him. He was friends with them - it was nice to see.

Without doubt, my father really only had one close friend that we knew of, Paddy Fox from Sunderland. I think that Paddy had been to school with him, but I'm not sure. It was such a lovely friendship they had. I think it transcended all the barriers of the showbusiness world. Paddy has never changed to this day and in lots of ways is still a 'Makem' from Sunderland, but a nicer bloke you couldn't hope to meet. The friendship between Paddy and my dad has been quite amazing - his house is still adorned with dad's pictures. Paddy is a lovely man, a bit of a rogue, and my dad would give him money because Paddy genuinely wanted nothing from my dad except his friendship. When it came to clothing, they were the same size except for shirts. As soon as dad was finished with a suit, Paddy got it... always. Paddy's wardrobe was full of dad's suits and even when dad died Paddy got the suits.

Everybody needs a friend, some one to associate with, that's what I think anyway, and that's what dad found in Paddy. The difference with Paddy was that he was both friend and servant. I will tell you a story. Paddy used to run to the bookies for dad and do all sorts. One day, my dad had some winnings to collect, say for arguments sake £100, but he sent Paddy to pick up the bet. When Paddy got to the bookies, they paid him out £100 too much - a mistake. When Paddy came back, he said they had paid him an extra £100. My father just said: 'Well, come on then, hand it over,' and Paddy handed over all the money. Instead of being sensible and just giving my dad the hundred quid, he handed over the lot. Dad just took it and gave him nowt for it - it was just expected. Paddy would do anything for my dad and even now he is fiercely protective of dad's memory. Clearly, they became exceptionally good friends and obviously got up to a lot together, as people do with their best friends. I think the reason why they were so close was because Paddy's mouth was shut. He was loyal in the extreme - maybe because he got up to just as much as my dad did....... The Sunshine Boys. Paddy would draw the line at other women because he was absolutely devoted to his wife, Rosie, who my dad held in nearly as high regard as Paddy. Dad looked after Paddy and Rosie well.

Holidays - I cannot remember how many times I took the four of them to Blackpool, and when I say the four of them I mean Paddy and Rosie, dad and A.N.Other - Lottie, Mary, Cissie. They only went away once together after he married Cissie. Most times, I would take them down and bring them back. I have seen him go to Blackpool with £2000 for a fortnight - you could go to the Bahamas with that for a month. He stayed at different small hotels, then it was always Len and Pat's place, the Prudhoe Hotel, in Lord Street - a small licensed guest house. The proprietors came from County Durham originally. The last I heard was that they had a larger place on the Promenade in Blackpool. Paddy and Rosie were never allowed to put their hands in their pockets once during the holiday, not even for the cups of tea they had when they stopped at a cafe just after breakfast. My dad wouldn't have had it any other way. At one time, my dad had thousands and thousands of pounds just lying around the house, but he still had to go to Blackpool for his holidays. It always made me laugh to read about him going to Majorca. He never went upstairs on a double decker bus, never mind an aeroplane. To my knowledge, he never went out of this country and didn't even have a passport. You have to remember that my dad loved the adulation, and there is only one place in the UK you can still get it, even when you're on holiday, and that's Blackpool. He tried Scarborough a few times and liked it, but it was too hilly, bad for his chest and nobody recognised him. Blackpool was the place. Everywhere they went, people knew him - it's full of Geordies - he loved it. When I drove him there, we stopped at Kirkby Stephen on the way and he'd more or less do a show in the café. All the buses would be stopped for a cup of tea and he'd be giving a show.

One year, he decided to have two holidays and, as usual, I was their driver. They had their holiday fortnight in Blackpool and were having another ten days in Scarborough. We stopped at a restaurant on the way. Give him his due, when you went out with dad he paid for everything and everyone knew him. He would wave to them and carry on and you would feel great, absolutely marvellous. But when it came to food, he was an awkward sod. Food in restaurants or motorway cafés is not the same as you get at home. I can remember buying something with boiled potatoes, and at the top of his voice he shouted: 'These tatties are not cooked - I'm not having these!' I just wanted to crawl away and die!

Paddy, Rosie, Lottie and my dad were true friends. If I won two hundred grand tomorrow, my status would change. I'd buy a bigger house and then my new neighbours would be the people I'd hang around with, whereas my dad's friends and contacts never changed. It didn't matter how much money he had, he kept the same friends. I'm not saying he was clever for doing that, perhaps it was ignorance.

You will have realised by now that, when it comes to my dad, my mind jumps around like a grasshopper. This is probably due to our early life-style as an entertainer's family, and the fact that I married at a reasonably young age and moved out of the family home. All of my recollections are in pieces rather than a continuous picture. It maybe easier if I touch upon different aspects of dad, like his habits, interests, character, beliefs, relationships etc. and record anything that comes to mind.

He was always very fussy about his appearance when he went out of the house. When he went to the bookies, which was every afternoon at one time, he'd have to be dressed from head to toe, suit - the lot. He used his lazy eye to good effect in his act, but he never thought about getting it corrected. Yet, he'd spend £500 for a suit and pay £1200 for a set of false teeth with transparent gums. Even then, he didn't use the bottom ones unless he was going out. He couldn't eat with them, so they used to stay on the sideboard.

Dad always smoked Woodbines and had done so since he was an eleven year old boy, when it was possible to buy a paper packet of two cigarettes. The Woodbine packet in his act has always been there because it's synonymous with drink and layabouts. He had always been a smoker, drinker and layabout. In fact, the hardest thing he did was look for nothing to do. He was probably too lazy. When he was on his own, he was too lazy to hoover the floor. The house was a tip. I'd say: 'Why not get this room papered?' 'What's the matter with the paper that's on?' was his reply. 'Why not get a new door on here?' 'The door opens and shuts doesn't it?' And he'd say it all in a funny sort of way and you'd laugh, but he really meant it. The place really was a tip and he could easily have bought something nice a hundred times over. Twice, Cissie sent my brother, Michael, with application forms for the council housing lists, but Michael was given £20 and instructions from my father to put the applications in the bin of The Ship pub at Whitley Bay. Cissie told me that she had applied for a council house, but I knew that Michael had carried out dad's orders.

Often, because of his lazy nature, he had to be cajoled to do things like shopping and sometimes we used to buy for him. I bought him patent leather shoes at Clinkard's and crocodile shoes from somewhere else - £70 for a pair of shoes (many years ago) - just like that.

Sometimes, you couldn't get him out of the house and then we would tell him that he simply had to get some new clothes - a couple of new suits. 'Oh, I'll get some, I'll get some,' was the response. Then suddenly, out of the blue, he would want to be out. Down he would go to Whitley Bay and order five suits at a time from John Collier's. He went there because there was no hassle. The manager would say: 'Hello, Bobby,' and my father would say: 'Right, I want one of them, one of them and one of them.' The bloke had his measurements and that was the end of the story. When they were ready, the man rang him up. My father would tell him to fetch them, then handed the money over. Sometimes, it swung the other way. He could go out and buy you a watch for no reason, for absolutely no reason. I have been sat in the house when he has given me £200. 'Get yourself something,' he would say, as if it was only 50 pence. Yet, at other times, you may have been down to see him and perhaps, on purpose, been saying: 'I don't know how I'm going to pay this electric bill,' and you would go out with not a bean. It goes back to the attitude that dad adopted when he bought drinks. If anybody hinted for a drink, he would go: 'Balls, I'm not sitting here buying...' and I can hear him saying it now... 'If he thinks I'm going to buy his drinks, he's got another think coming!' And yet, if somebody was to say: 'Can I get you a drink, Bobby, let me get them,' he would say: 'You're bloody not, I'm getting the drinks.'

One incident stays very clearly in my mind. I was at the house one day and Michael said: 'Have you seen what my dad has given me?' It was a £3000 gold Rolex watch. It was my dad's watch. I said: 'Bloody hell, what have I done?' 'Oh,' my dad said: 'I've got something for you, as well,' and he takes a sovereign ring off his finger - spontaneously. It wasn't for me at all. I said: 'Thanks very much.' You couldn't take offence at that, but he used to be very, very nasty and then I'd stay away for days and I'd get Michael on the phone saying he was still on his high horse. It was usually about nothing, just depression if life had got him down. There may well have been something specific in his mind, like women or money troubles, but he wouldn't discuss it. Then out of the blue, for no reason, he would ring me up to say: 'Will you come down, I've got something for you?' When I arrived he would say: 'There's fifty quid, go and have yourself a drink.' However, you could go to see him at Christmas and not even get a card. This was due to his moodiness, which got worse as he got older, and I'm not sure to this day why he was like that. The stage was really his whole life and I think that it was a release for him to be up there. He became very introverted and stopped smiling unless he was performing. It is sad that he had to have an illness before dying, as it would have been a fitting finale for him to die suddenly on stage. The Bobby Thompson that the public saw was nothing like the Bobby Thompson we saw. The miserable side, the mistrust. Even though he had money, he wouldn't buy a house. Although he spent money on clothes, he would only wear them when he was on official duty.

If you took a present to my dad, he wouldn't open it - he might open it a few days later. Christmas Day - he wouldn't even get out of bed. If you have children, it's a great pleasure on Christmas Day watching them open their presents. The pleasure is in giving not getting. My dad's only pleasure was in giving money. He wouldn't think about going out to buy anything, he would give you a tenner. My mother used to buy Christmas presents and things. He would give us things that he possessed, like that sovereign ring. He had two grandchildren and was just as unpredictable with them. Even though he liked them, he didn't display a lot of affection, but then he didn't show much to us either. Sometimes, he did with us, but he wasn't a touching, loving father, and he wasn't an affectionate grey-haired grandfather. One day, he said to my kids: 'Here's £500, book a holiday.' On other days, when it was their birthday, he wouldn't even give them a pound. It just depended how the mood took him. He would either be as nice as pie to them or sit as miserable as sin, drink his tea and not open his mouth. It was always the same with his immediate family. When my children were younger, they used to go and count his money out of the safe for him. He wouldn't let them open the pay packets, but he'd stack them up and they'd count the pound notes. The pleasure they got was in counting the money - as kids would. On his living-room floor they would have piles of pennies and fifty pences etc. As they grew older, my children liked the idea of having a famous grandad and my daughter has his sense of humour, but they didn't go around telling anyone who their grandfather was. He was very unpredictable and capable of big swings in mood. I don't think anybody, with the possible exception of my mother, knew my dad. We would know, sometimes, how to manoeuvre him, if you like, but that was all.

Dad was only relaxed in his own home where he liked to be slovenly. He rarely relaxed in terms of speech or conversation. His interests were few: he read his paper, placed his bets, went to races and watched TV, particularly sports. My father was a particularly squeamish man - the sight of blood or violence of any kind used to distress him terribly, which was surprising since he was an avid boxing fan. I suppose it was because he thought the violence in the ring was controlled and not leading to anyone else's distress.

He didn't like cruelty to children and I remember him sitting in his chair, next to the cupboard, saying: 'Bastard!' when it showed a man on TV being jailed for abusing a child. Although he could be very emotional, and would often cry at news reports on television, he never showed great passion. He was never an inveterate swearer - every other word wasn't a swear word, but he'd swear if he got into a paddy. Often, he swore and he didn't realise he was doing it - he would call you a whore or a bastard, but wouldn't mean it. 'You soft looking bastard, you.' Having said that, he would fiercely protect you in front of somebody else - even though he wouldn't give you the same reverence to your face.

Although he had the sovereign rings and the expensive bracelet, he couldn't cut it with people who showed their wealth, people with dark glasses, people with gold-rimmed glasses - it was illogical, but he disliked rich people. He would look at people and say: 'Aa divven't like him (or her)' - and he wouldn't. People used to approach him for all sorts of things. If he thought you were all right - not what the scheme was - then you had a chance. But if you came in with a £500 suit and a pair of gold-rimmed glasses, then you were knackered - no chance.

Dad was certainly capable of friendship and genuine kindness. He had a friend, Norman Finnegan, whom he had known from school, and Norman's brother was Mayor of Sunderland. On many occasions, my father used to bring Norman to the house, feed him and let him stop the night.

After his marriage in 1982, Paddy and Rosie didn't see as much of dad as they used to, so I tried to make it up to them by going to see them and giving them a few pictures. Their home has my dad's photos all over. Recently, Rosie rang to ask if I was going to come along and surprise Paddy on his birthday. I couldn't think what to give him, but I had my dad's last CIU club card with eleven paid up year passes. Obviously, I wanted to keep it, but the bloke had been my dad's friend for nearly forty years. I wrapped the card and gave it to him as a present. The poor man broke down in tears. You would think that I had given him a couple of grand. He said to me: 'I could write a book. Me and your dad go back a long way, and I wouldn't dare tell Rosie about some of the things that happened.' Paddy was sound in the knowledge that he had been closer to my dad than anyone. I was a little bit annoyed that my dad had dropped his friends after marriage, but they came back. They had been close friends for such a long time, been on holidays together, shared lodgings, bad times and good times. Paddy was my dad's dresser on every big night, but he wasn't there all of the time. He would have stretches of up to three months when he would be with my dad every night. Paddy ran after my dad like a servant. Paddy and Rosie saw dad's other women - they would all go out in a foursome - Paddy, Rosie, dad and Madame X, whoever she might be at the time. They used to come and stay for three or four week spells until my dad said that it was time for them to go. He'd ring them and tell them he was sending a taxi through to pick them up from their Sunderland home. After a few days, Paddy and Rosie would say: 'Eeh, we'll have to go - we have to see the milkman on Thursday.' Dad would tell them that they weren't going and send a taxi through to see to their milkman. That is what he was like when he was on song.

In my opinion, he made his last wife's life quite miserable. Dad had, that I know of, numerous other women. He'd go to the casino every night and a good few afternoons. I'm not a gambler and would go to the casino perhaps twice a year, just to see him and have a chat. There would always be women hanging around him and he'd always have somebody on his arm. I believe that his last marriage was born out of loneliness because I had left home and Michael was rarely there. His routine would consist of getting up at 1.00pm, having breakfast and then going out to the Casino Royale, where he would stay until 5.00am the next morning. Breakfast would be eaten at the casino, before he returned home to sleep and start the cycle all over again. My father was quite a lonely man.

There were various spots of trouble. He was twice physically attacked. Once, there was an incident in Hartlepool where he got a black eye. We never got to the bottom of it, but I'm convinced that a woman was involved because no one else would want to hit my dad. I've never met anyone, apart from agents and close associates, who ever had a wrong word for him. Even then, it was because he was cantankerous and difficult with money. In another incident, he was punched outside a book-makers, Ladbroke's, in Park View, Whitley Bay. After that incident, I went down with him to the shop, but we never found out why it happened. Again, I'm convinced it was due to a woman because he wasn't mugged or anything like that.

He had girl friends during the time he was engaged to Mary Douglas, and during the time he had Cissie as a live-in housekeeper, he was seeing a lady called Mabel. She would ring me, to ask him to ring her. Mabel was absolutely dotty on him. She wanted to marry dad, but he wasn't interested in marriage. He wanted to see her because he liked the woman. He had cut Mabel off when he got engaged to Mary, but she came back. Mary was Lottie Tate's sister. She came on the scene after Lottie died, but I suspect that he had been seeing her before then. Anyway, not long after Lottie's death, they got engaged. The reason Mary went out of his life was that she wanted him to move, buy a house and spend a lot of money. We were all in favour, as we wanted them to have a little bit of comfort in life, but shortly afterwards she asked my dad for a big loan for her son to take up the tenancy of a pub. My dad had no intention of lending his own kids any money, let alone somebody else's. The engagement went right out of the window. I think it was purely because she had said the words 'will you give me' and not 'do you want'.

His attraction for women could create jealousy. One evening, in a Killingworth club, I can remember a group of girls on a hen night. There were about five or six of them and they couldn't have been more than seventeen or eighteen. One or two came over and sat on my dad's knee. They were stroking his head, asking for autographs and just being generally silly. Not unnaturally, Cissie didn't like their behaviour and from that day on, as far as I know, she wouldn't allow my dad to sign any autographs for women. She signed the autographs. She got photographs and signed them 'Best Wishes, Cissie and Bobby Thompson'. Yes, dad was revered and idolised by lots of people, but by women in particular. I really think it was because they wanted to mother him. I cannot believe that it was because of his looks or sexual prowess. When it came to women, anyone who came up to him, who was attractive and nicely dressed, took him aback, and his way out of it was to be off-hand. He liked them, but probably felt insecure - even though a lot of them were genuinely quite attracted to him. You look at somebody like the hypnotist, Tony Sands, who used to work quite a lot with dad. Now, Tony was 'Mr Smooth': white beard, grey hair brushed back, dark glasses, £5000 diamond ring, £1000 diamond watch. He looked absolutely superb, but my dad used to take the mickey out of him something awful. They got on well together. Both of them would attract the extremely good looking females, but whereas Tony could talk to them in the same way as any other fans, my dad would be frightened off by them. I don't know about all the women my dad was involved with, but I don't think that he ever resorted to call-girls, he didn't need to.

Certainly, he was waited on hand and foot by all of his ladies. I can remember him saying to Cissie: 'I'll have my breakfast now.' Two minutes later it was there. Or: 'I'll have a cup of tea.' Not: 'Will you give me' or 'Can I have'. They'd go running around after him without a moment's hesitation. Michael and he had vicious arguments at one time because Michael wouldn't wait on him. He used to do messages and bits and pieces, but Michael wouldn't do them if my dad tried to snap his fingers and order him about as he did with Lottie and Cissie. Dad was always smart when Lottie was there. She used to iron his clothes and they would always be ready for him. He would come down the stairs and they'd be hanging from the picture rail in the hall, ready for him to carry into the living room to get changed. All that seemed to alter in his later years. Whether it was because he got older, or whether it was the loss of Lottie's touch, I don't know.

Dad's hands were impeccable, his nails were cut perfectly, his face clean shaven - my dad's shaving was an art. His hair was immaculate, but from the neck down he would be absolutely rotten. He'd wear the same long-johns for a fortnight and go into the bath once every ten days. Even on his video, you can see him changing, with his long-johns on, and the camera suddenly takes a step back. He would laugh whenever we suggested that he should have a bath and say that he'd only been in the bath on Sunday. But this would be the following Tuesday, eight days later. Dad was a hypochondriac. He would take three or four Anadin tablets twice a day in case he got a headache. He drank a bottle of Angier's Emulsion every two days. He drank Benylin cough mixture. You never told him that he didn't look well otherwise he would be reporting to the Coroner's Court. He took anything and everything in the way of patent medicines. At one time, he coughed up a bit of blood - it was probably tomato skin - and for weeks afterwards he wouldn't go near a club. Later on, of course, he was genuinely ill and couldn't go to the clubs. There were periods in his life when he just wouldn't take on work. Any normal working person would be saying: 'I've got to go to work,' but my dad wouldn't, he was too big for that. In many ways, he thought that he was too big for the clubs because he could pick and choose his work. He even rang up clubs where he was booked to perform and said: 'I want a seat near the front and if there's no seat then I'm not coming.' It's just the way that he was, he was in complete control. He commanded a separate table for himself and his guests at every place - he had them running around after him. I suppose it is a bit like the women film stars of today - everything they want they get and he used to get it too.

The control extended to his act. At the end of the day, he had them laughing before he opened his mouth. They knew exactly what he was going to say and laughed before he said it. On the other hand, in the home, he could be mean, hard, totally different - perhaps even schizophrenic. He was very keen on snooker and played in a Pro-Am tournament with Steve Cram and Jimmy White at Eldon Square. Jimmy White's father won a prize of a television set and my dad was absolutely convinced that it was a fiddle. I wouldn't care, but he shook Jimmy White's hand and his father's and said what a pleasure it was to see them, and how delighted he was that Jimmy White's dad had won something and all the rest of it. We walked out of the door and he said: 'It's a blinking fix.' It is just the way that he was, he mistrusted everybody.

He was an avid Sunderland supporter, which didn't go down well with me because I'm a Newcastle season ticket holder. We used to have friendly banter about it in the house. Dad was a friend of Squadron Leader Jimmy Rush, a Newcastle United director, and was his guest on a number of occasions in the director's box. He was also a friend of Tom Cowie and Jack Charlton and went to Sunderland and Leeds to see matches. As well as horse-racing, dog-racing was another interest and he was privileged to be a member of Postal Turf Services. Only the rich and famous are allowed accounts there, which means that you can just pick up the phone and bet up to £500 at a time. It didn't do him any good, mind you. Dad had no real hobbies at all. When he had a night off, I took him to various pubs and clubs in the area. This was a bit off-putting for some of the turns because more people would be looking at dad than at them. He did little socialising other than spending so much time at the Casino Royale. When the casino opened, it was like a whole new lease of life for him and he made it his home. He would go there around 11.00 pm and stay until 5.00 am - every night, week in and week out. He got to know everybody in the place and they were delighted to have him because he drew other people in. Although there were some famous people patronising the casino, my dad was the focal point and he loved that as much as the actual gambling. But then again, they didn't see the true side of him. He was politeness itself to them. Dad seemed to be genuine in his feelings for the owner, Homer Michaelides, of whom he always spoke well - which was unusual because he was mostly two-faced about people. He could be the most charming man you could wish to meet, but his language could be absolutely atrocious. He could wipe the floor with agents as if they didn't matter, as if they weren't human beings. This was simply because he mistrusted everyone and believed that they were out to take his money from him.

Money put a gap between my father and myself. I often felt that I wasn't his son because there was a lot of favouritism shown to my brother. I might have been wrong and I realise that. Michael and I were slightly different - he was always a bit more hard-up because he spent more. Michael lived at home and I didn't. Michael liked to gamble and drink and dad gave him around £20 a day pocket-money. I found the unequal treatment disconcerting. However, I was working for myself and had a car and a decent business. Dad liked the car, which he thought was for carrying him around. That was another thing, I used to drive my dad all over the place and I mean all over the place. Lunch-time, from Whitley Bay up to the casino - he would give me a tenner. Then I would pick him up and take him back home and he'd give me another tenner. I felt embarrassed taking the money, but it made him feel good and I'm sure that he felt that he was achieving something. At one stage, Lottie suggested that perhaps I wasn't his son after all. On reflection, it's probably very unlikely, but who knows?

He never helped me financially. A long time ago, when I worked in the steel industry, my father loaned me £4000 to set up a business on my own. He asked for the money back about six weeks later. I had to give it to him - it was par for the course - he thought that I had spent it. I had a car, you see, which I bought on hire purchase, a loan from the bank and my dad's four grand. Of course, I rolled up in the car to pick him up and it was: 'Where did you get this?'

'I bought it.'

'What with?'

'I took a loan out.'

'Oh, aye?'

A fortnight later, he asked for his money back: 'I need that money.'

'What do you need the money for, dad?'

'I've had some heavy expenses, I need the money back, can you get it today?' I had to give it back the following day. You couldn't fall out with him, but I had made the mistake of showing him that I had a car. Of course, what he thought was that I had taken the four grand and bought a car, which was not the case.

Sometimes, he was just a bloody liar. When I had the fish and chip business, it was really fantastic. My partner, Alec Beecham, and I built it up from nothing. A lot of people thought it was done with my dad's money, but it wasn't - Alec had the cash. We had oak beams, Georgian panels round the walls, terrazzo floors. It was better than a house. Alec and I (together with some lads who were working for me at the time) did everything. We got planning permission, bought and installed a second-hand range, did the fittings, everything. We even had special brown wrapping paper with pictures of Friar Tuck eating our fish and chips. My dad came along to open the restaurant for us (I advertised it as Bobby Thompson opening the place.) He came along, shook my hand and talked to me as if I were Joe Public off the street or a businessman client. He even asked me to pay for a taxi for him there and back, which I thought was a bit peculiar. A few weeks later, when I was in the Casino Royale and talking to this bloke about the business, dad came up and introduced an acquaintance to me. 'This is my son, Keith.' The man said: 'Oh, yes, I've just read an article about you in the newspaper. You've got the fish and chip shop in Whitley Bay, haven't you?' My dad just turned round and said: 'Yes, I've set him up in that and it's doing well.' He hadn't put in one penny, but he wanted people to think that he was there in the background somewhere.

I can always remember that, wherever we went, our family was the life and soul of the party. It could have been ridicule that we attracted - I don't know - but wherever my dad was, that was the centre of activity. Going around shopping with him in Whitley Bay, on the rare occasions that we did, was like walking around with Santa Claus. I remember going into a Whitley Bay jeweller's shop. The manager came over and asked: 'What can we get for you, Mr Thompson?' Dad said: 'Hey, it's Bob, divvent call me Mr Thompson - have you got any second-hand bracelets?' Everybody was laughing as they thought he was joking, but he wasn't. He wanted a decent second-hand bracelet. He bought this gold identity bracelet for about £1600 and Cissie said that he later pawned it. Going into another jeweller's shop, on a different occasion, we saw this gold bracelet for about £400 - £500 - it was a charm bracelet for Lottie. I went in there a few times with him and he would say to me, in front of the man in the shop: 'Do you want something? Just get whatever you want.' Of course, I said: 'No.' Had I said: 'Yes,' he would have had a heart attack. It was all show for the man, so some one could say what a generous person Bobby Thompson was - but he knew all along that you wouldn't say 'Yes.'

In the streets, everybody would be looking at you, but it wasn't embarrassing, it was nice, you felt important. People would come up every five minutes. 'Bobby, can you remember when I was in this club or that club?' 'Can you remember when I did this or that?' And my dad had them all convinced that he knew them personally. He'd say: 'Hello, Sunshine, how are you?' when in reality he'd never seen them in his life. I'd say to him: 'Who was that?' and he'd say: 'Eeh, aa divvent knaa.' Somebody would come up and say: 'Do you remember that night in South Shields Victory Club?' and my dad would say: 'Eeh, aye, what a night we had.' Then when the bloke was gone, he'd say that he had never seen him in his life. I like to think that he was just kind to people, but maybe he just played his public. The man was too deep for me to understand, let alone the public. During this conversation I find myself thinking, did I even know this bloke?

I can't remember being told off, other than after I was married when I did daft things. He took much more interest in Michael's career. Michael was a book-maker, after he left the Civil Service, and therefore they had something to talk about. When Michael was working at the betting shop he got calls from dad. 'What's the price on this?' 'What's the price on that?' 'What's happening?' 'Have you put the bet on?' Of course, Michael was a professional book-maker because he could reckon up bets without paper or calculator as most book-makers can. Dad would be firing questions at him every ten minutes and Michael would lose his temper and say: 'For Christ's sake, father, don't ring me anymore, you only rang me a few minutes ago!' Michael is homosexual, self-confessed, and my father knew that, but never wanted to admit it. Because Michael was gay, I think my dad felt that he needed more looking after than me and they had a very close bond. Dad used to call homosexuals 'nancy-boys' which was the old-fashioned term. My recollection of that was in the Fifties when he got rid of his agents. One of them was very friendly with Michael who used to stay at his house. I didn't think anything of it at the time because we were quite young, but looking back I'm sure that's why he left their agency. Michael held all dad's secrets - all the ones my dad wanted to hold from the women in his life. Michael was privy to everything and would deliver messages to people and, in return, my dad would give him money.

Without being unkind, that was the major fault that my dad had, he thought everyone wanted money. Whenever he wanted anybody to do anything, he felt that he had to offer them a few quid. He embarrassed me something awful at my wedding by giving the bride's father a ten pound note. I can remember my wife's father being most upset. Dad wasn't being charitable or awful, he just thought that everybody wanted money from him. He saw that as normal. 'Here's a few quid, get yourself a drink,' he would say. Anyone's reaction would have been: 'I don't want your money.' He mistrusted everybody - even his own family.

As I think I have mentioned earlier, if ever you wanted money for anything, there was always suspicion. In his mind, you always wanted it for reasons other than those you gave him. I can recall borrowing £50 to book a holiday, not because I didn't have the money, but because I didn't have it on me. The next day, he asked if I had made the booking. When I told him that I hadn't, he went berserk, saying that I had got the money under false pretences - it was like being at school. He had a phobia about people taking him for a ride. He didn't come to physical blows, but he came to verbal ones with Brian Shelley every other day because he felt that as Brian, as an agent, was picking up more money than he should be. I don't know why he was like that. He used to come home from playing roulette in Newcastle and say that the tables were rigged, and he knew this because the man who owned it was making too much money. Of course, it was nonsense. Even with the records, from which he made a fortune, he felt that he never got fully paid. I think that he was the world's best liar, he was absolutely stupendous at lying and had people crying for him sometimes.

He wasn't the fool that he appeared to be. Dad wasn't a scholar, but when it came to the crunch he knew exactly how many fingers he had on each hand. Certainly, he wouldn't let anyone put one over on him. Having said that, he had a number of false friends. It would go through stages. There was a fellow who used to be the manager of a North-East night-club. None of the family liked this man and no one else seemed to like him, but he hung on with my dad for ages and ages. He had a number of these people throughout his life, but I can't remember him being close with any celebrities. A number of local turns used to ring him up, but his mistrust extended to them as well, probably because he feared that they might achieve more success than him. No comedian on television was ever any good unless he spoke to them face to face. If he was speaking to them personally, it was different. I can remember him speaking to a TV household name and saying what an absolutely wonderful act he was, that he was brilliant and the best thing that he had ever seen. I distinctly recall him putting the phone down and saying to me: 'That bloke's a bundle of shite, he's not fit to be on.' That was my dad - you laugh at it afterwards, but he meant it. On the other hand, he took no delight in recalling that he had once been brought in to replace Gerry Dorsey (later Engelbert Humperdinck) mid-week at a North-East night-club.

One person he disliked was Bobby Pattinson. There was no question about it and nothing could change his mind. This was inspite of the fact that he had been very fond of Bobby Pattinson's mother, who used to run a concert party in my dad's younger days. He mistrusted Tyne Tees TV and you would try to tell him that a company like that was too big to do underhand things and rip him off, but he wouldn't accept it - everyone was out to rob him. Dad didn't trust banks, that's why he kept most of his money in a safe. He could be very astute with money in some ways, but unfortunately, in later years, gambling took over in a big way and he spent vast amounts of money. About ten or twelve years ago, I remember seeing in dad's safe about £80,000 in unopened pay packets. In my opinion, that was certainly spent within two or three years at the Casino Royale in Newcastle.

Dad had a completely different life-style in his later years - certainly more respectable. The success of his record albums made a lot of difference. When he first made the records, he thought it was going to be no use at all. He struck up a deal, through Brian Shelley, with David Wood of the Impulse Sound Studios in Wallsend. My dad made an absolute fortune. He used to get cheques of £30-40,000 at a time. He got two gold discs and I think that each gold disc marks £200,000 worth of sales. One of those discs hangs in my son's bedroom.

Whatever people say about my dad, he did a lot for charities, but always thought that they were trying to put one over on him. 'I'm sick of charity do's,' he'd say. Someone in his position gets asked to do something every day of the week. If it is not someone wanting to do an interview during the day, then it's some organisation wanting him to do a charity performance at night. Dad was keen on boys' clubs and miners' charities. He did two charities for Joe Gormley, who was then President of the NUM, and a number of shows for the Aged Miners' Welfare Fund. Every year, for ten years, he opened the St. Mary's Mental

Hospital Fete at Stannington, Northumberland. He was quite a close friend of the parish priest, Father Cass, who would come to our home often. Dad liked to think that he was a good Catholic and would willingly do anything for Catholic charities. He gave a lot of money to The Little Sisters of The Poor.

He turned down jobs. I can remember stars of the past being paid large fees for playing the High Pit Social Club at Cramlington and not filling the place. My dad was supposed to appear there a month or so after these 'big names', and the place was sold out well in advance. However, my dad was being paid something like half of the fee that these one time big acts were receiving. When he asked them to explain why, when he could sell out a house, he was on less money, they fell out and he refused to go on. My dad was only once threatened with legal action for not appearing. It was at a night club in Washington Galleries. He had gone there, took one look at the steps he had to climb (I think that there were five flights) and said: 'I ain't going in there,' got back into the car and went home. They decided to take him to court for something like £700 and he had Basil Mellon, of Gateshead, as his brief. Basil was a tough nut in legal terms. He sent them one letter and they didn't take it any further. Although dad was a humble man, deep down he was rooted to the idea that he was number one and the best. He was determined that he was going to be treated as the best and didn't want to be mucked around by anyone.

Going back a long time to the early days, my father had one or two bluish jokes in his act which he got rid of. He once had a business card printed 'Bobby Thompson, North-East Comedian - Clean and Clever', which was quite nice. He made a big thing of not being dirty and for a long time had a running battle with Bernard Manning, whose act could be so blue. Their battle got into the papers, with Bernard saying that Bobby Thompson was just a comedian from a hick town etc, and my father saying that Bernard Manning could only make a living as a comedian by being blue. I can remember dad talking about Roy 'Chubby' Brown and saying that he was one of the most brilliant young comedians. Brown at that time was probably on £40 a night. A year or so later, his dialogue changes to four letter words and he's on £1,500 a night. A man has his family to support, so what is he supposed to do? But my dad thought that he was above that - although he could swear like a trooper in the house. He might have been jealous of their success, but I think that he was genuine. How many comedians could use the same material and costume for thirty years and never lose popularity - but my dad did. He conned everybody, didn't he?

He was definitely not conceited, but neither was he surprised by his success. Frequently, I would say: 'How did you go down last night?' He'd say: 'Absolutely brilliant.' There were some clubs whose atmosphere he didn't like. He really hated to play the Downhill Club, Sunderland, even though he was regarded as a Sunderland lad. Funnily enough, he always went down well at that club, but he'd still be nervous every time he had to appear there because of its reputation as a graveyard for comedians. High Pit was another club that he was not struck on, whether it was because of the trouble I mentioned earlier I don't know. Like everything else, some clubs have a reputation for making you feel welcome and some don't. Others have reputations for poor audiences.

There were times in his career when he appeared on club 'Go As You Pleases' and wasn't placed. It must have affected his confidence. I never saw him on stage when he was down on his luck, but I booked him once for a Boys' Club charity event at Percy Main Club, North Shields. The place was absolutely heaving. Gifts had come in from all over and my dad had also donated some money. I was frightened to death, but when he came on stage I was moved and proud. People laughed heartily and it was nice to witness that reaction. He could make me laugh as I inherited, or developed, a similar kind of humour. Even today, I use some of his jokes and also his phrases like 'give ower'. People say that I sound like him when I use his words, but I don't mean to copy him in any way - it's just that I find the phrases funny. For instance, the ones he used in the joke where the judge turns round and says: 'Can you settle out of court?' and the policeman repeats : 'Can you settle out of court?' and Bobby says: 'Give him the breathalyser.' Everybody knows what he means and laughs. I use that kind of thing now. I'm particularly proud that no one has taken his material. I don't know whether they would be able to or not. It's a tribute, really. I've been with him on many occasions and was at the Mayfair, Newcastle, when James Whale presented him with a plaque to mark fifty years in showbusiness. Spike Rawlings and Brian Lewis were there. Dad had four retirement do's that I know of, and made a few bob out of them, which I find quite funny. He never had any intention of retiring. It was usually somebody else's idea that he just went along with. 'Forty years in showbusiness', 'fifty years in showbusiness', 'Bobby Thompson's last night at the Mayfair' - I think he had twelve last nights at the Mayfair.

I'm only sad that, having had such a great reputation for so many years, at the end of his career his act was so poor due to ill health. When I talk to friends, they will say: 'Oh, he wasn't the same when he played our club.' Comments like that hurt me, but he was lucky that everyone remembered what he was. You have got to remember him for two things. First, the ordinary act where he did the everyday routine like 'Give him the breathalyser' - quite a modern joke and later updated to 'Is he on glue?' Secondly, my father's army sketch - the most brilliant thing. Nothing else done by anyone else compares with it. It was his idea - the bit about the Queen and Hitler - all his own invention. He had probably done the act since the war. It is the kind of stuff you tell your mates: 'Oh, I've just seen Hitler at the fish shop.'

It was never a big deal for my dad to go on stage. Some artists are tense, but it didn't bother him. Normally, dad would turn up at a club about quarter to eight in the evening. He'd start to get ready at home, around quarter to seven, by washing his hands and face and then shaving. He dyed his hair everyday with Inector, using a little toothbrush to scrub it into the roots, because his hair was lily-white, but to everyone else it was thick-black. He'd be ready and waiting for the taxi at quarter past seven and would troop off to reach the club for quarter to eight. It is fair to say that he was extremely punctual and I suppose that is where his timing comes in. He was rarely late for any appointment or job, but was totally disorganised in everything else. He could have made and kept a fortune, but he kept no records. At one time in his career, clubs would ring him up and ask him to turn up for a date and he would agree. However, his agent, Brian Shelley, would already have booked him out elsewhere and as a result some club would be let down. In the early days, he did that because he was offered more money, but in later years it was because he was disorganised.

He remained accessible to a certain degree. People could always come and talk to him and he was pleasant, even if he was in a bad mood. He loved the adulation and he loved the fans. I have never seen him refuse an autograph or give anyone the brush-off. Everybody 'knew' him. I suppose it's like when you sit next to a celebrity - you have seen them on screen and therefore feel as if you know them - but you don't. The public felt as if they knew my dad and of course very few people did - very few.

Later in life, he really couldn't sing - it was pitiful and if he had simply been a singer he would have been booed off. However, when he sang those emotional songs like "HMS Hood", after his turn, people used to sway their arms in the air and sing along with him, even though he sounded lousy. He could bring tears to their eyes - he couldn't sing, but they loved it. He just needed to play the opening bars of "Beautiful Dreamer" or "Sweet Sixteen" on his harmonica and the audience would start to sing it from their seats, their voices getting louder and louder. I don't know whether it was because they appreciated his humour so much, but it was quite moving to be there and watch them singing along. They were even quiet at the bar. It was weird. He regarded himself as a romantic singer and wouldn't sing anything raunchy or loud. Occasionally, he would ask us how he sounded singing a particular song. I can remember bursting out laughing and saying: 'For heaven's sake, dad.' There were a number of comedy songs, written by Eric Boswell, which he recorded, but they haven't been released. They are about the races and that sort of thing, but he doesn't sound right on them and I won't release them. He was at his best when he was singing ballads. Lousy, but at his best and loving it. He thought that he could sing, that was the peculiar thing. Picture the scene. Dad, in costume, singing this emotional song and then, with the last note, sticking his arms in the air, and everyone going berserk. For somebody who can't sing, it has to be either the ultimate 'con' or just blind love for my dad. Really, I think they just loved him. When he sang "I'm Nobody's Child", I wanted to hide in a hole somewhere and cringe. Yet, by the time he had finished, the audience was singing along with him, swaying from side to side - unbelievable. We used to get a lot of scripts and songs (one titled "Sunday Scranchunes" sticks vividly in my mind) through the post for my dad to consider. They were usually sent by fans and were mostly terrible - he never used any of them.

I often get asked about my dad's stage clothes. Regarding the Little Waster costume, I remember having a jumper that Mammy Green knitted for me when we lived in her home at Barley Mow. I think it was a green cycling jumper with a polo neck, stripe around the middle and two different colours on the top. He used that jumper, which I think was the original, regularly until it was stolen around 1960. The replacement jumper was one knitted by a lady fan from The Ship, Monkseaton and he picked it to bits in places before using it. The trousers were a pair of his old plus-twos or fours from one of his suits and the cap was his own. The army uniform came from the Durham Light Infantry. A bloke gave him that uniform - I think that dad had done a couple of shows for them. The second jumper is at least thirty years old, the trousers are older and the army uniform is probably older than that again. To my knowledge, the Little Waster costume has never been washed for fourteen years. You can smell the Woodbines when you open the carrying case. Some years ago, I actually donated the clothes, but it was a mistake, I realise that now. I gave them to Radio Metro for a charity auction. A local comedian offered £1,000 for them, but Giles Squire wrote to me saying that it might not be in the best of taste to auction them and would I like to reconsider. I rang him, thanked him, and said that with hindsight he was probably right and that I'd hang onto them. It was very nice of him and a sensible gesture. He sent me a lovely letter saying that he had worked with my dad and that he was a credit to the North-East.

Over the years, I have seen my father carry out lots of important engagements and although national exposure, through his appearance on 'Wogan', came too late, this was, in my opinion (although not my dad's), one of the main highlights. The BBC put him up at an expensive London hotel and I think that one of Wogan's chauffeured cars met him at the station because he wouldn't fly. He got into the hotel and went down to the bar for a sandwich, and it was something ludicrous like £3.50. My dad threw it back across the bar and said: 'I'm not paying £3. 10. 0d (he still thought and talked in old money) for a skittering sandwich wi' no crust.' He genuinely meant it. He wasn't being funny, he simply wasn't going to pay that amount for a sandwich when he felt he was being ripped-off. Dad was out of his depth, or rather away from his roots.

We had all stayed back at work to see the Wogan show, about forty or fifty of us. When he started off, he was very slow and the audience were unappreciative. I began to get embarrassed and go red. It was embarrassment for him as well, as I thought that he was going to flop, but by the end of seven or eight minutes he had won them over. He proved to be quite a success and they were cheering. But when Terry Wogan was actually talking to him, he was really like an old man and seemed unable to converse properly. It came too late for him and he didn't give a jot. It was rumoured that he received a fantastic fee, but in fact he received £250, which I understand was the standard amount. I'm not even sure why he agreed to appear. Terry Wogan had an agent up here - I think it was a girl at Sunderland - and I understand that she mentioned that it would be a good idea to have this comedian, who was a living legend in the North, as a guest. After a research team had followed him around and watched his act at four or five clubs, they asked him if he would like to be on the show. In fairness, dad didn't jump at the offer. His initial reaction was: 'London ? It's a long way to go, what's the point?' BBC fees were poor, something he knew from past experience. In addition to the £250 fee, he got expenses, but when he came back he said: 'I'm not doing that again. I'm not going back there for this money.'

He actually backed out of a London Palladium charity show - perhaps it was lack of money, as it is not easy to fill a theatre like the Palladium, or perhaps he didn't like the supporting acts. He wasn't really bothered about national stardom. When you think about it, he didn't need it. He had all the money he ever needed from shows up here. Whether or not he was telling the truth I don't know, but he always insisted that he was loyal to the North-East clubland because the clubs had stuck with him through thick and thin. I can't tell you if he believed that, as I can't remember him being genuine too often, but he must have been sincere on some matters.

In his life, he knew a lot of important and famous people. There wasn't a mayor that he didn't know. He knew the mayors of Blyth, Newcastle and Sunderland and he knew them all on first name terms. One Sunday, I was at his house, and he was talking about this bloke that he'd met at Tyne Tees TV studios the week before, on a New Year's Eve show. It came out that he had been talking to Bob Geldof. He said: 'I don't know what he does, but he must be quite important because they were running around after him.' I thought: 'Christ', you know. This was just after the time that Bob Geldof had done the Ethiopian Appeal. Dad just took the meeting for granted - he wasn't overawed. All these people he simply took in his stride. And he is to be commended in a lot of ways because he hung onto his roots and never felt inferior to anyone.

My father wasn't illiterate, but he certainly couldn't construct a letter or anything of that nature. He never had a script of any kind, but relied on his memory. It's rather like somebody who works in a book-makers and isn't a good mathematician but is just brilliant with bets. Well, dad was like that with jokes, he could reel them off one after the other. The more laughter and response he got, the more his adrenalin and jokes flowed. If things went badly with an audience, he couldn't remember them. He never went down badly with an audience except towards the end when he couldn't remember, couldn't speak properly and could hardly climb the stairs in some of the clubs. I suppose it became embarrassing, but how do you tell a man (who has two gold discs, probably earned two million pounds and has known fantastic success) that he is not successful anymore when people are still paying £2 and £3 in clubs to see his show? It is just not possible.

He rarely confided in me. The only thing of importance in his life that he ever discussed with me was the bankruptcy proceedings, and that was because I went to court with him. I think that I set his mind at rest when I said to him: 'Look, whatever money you've got is in cash, isn't it?' He said: 'Yes.' 'And you don't owe anybody anything?' 'No.' 'OK,' I said, 'that's all you need to worry about because you are going to be no worse off after you come out of court than you were when you went into it.' And that was absolutely true because he didn't owe anybody any money. 'Who is going to jail Bobby Thompson, a 75 year old comedian?' I asked him. 'If you come out of court and you still owe them £120,000 and have the money in your pocket, you'll be a hero.' Sure enough, he was a hero. The examiner at his bankruptcy hearing actually smiled at him and said: 'Have a seat.' In my opinion, he was more abrupt with the tax-man's brief than with my dad. I remember the brief had said to dad: 'Are you Robert Michael Thompson?' and the examiner interrupted and said: 'Yes, yes, we can all see who it is, thank you, just get on with it.' I thought that to be absolutely rich. He got off rather lightly. To this day, he never paid a penny of that back. Royalties from £300,000 worth of sales, from Tyne Tees TV videos, have gone to the family. He's avoided paying the tax-man even after death. There was nobody in court covering the bankruptcy and it was only reported a couple of weeks later because dad told them. He seriously didn't think of going to jail because he could not have taken it, but they wouldn't have put him in jail. As much as he might have deserved it, they wouldn't have done it. But if anyone owes £120,000 in tax, they've probably earned it, haven't they? And by heavens, he earned it.

Dad never bothered with doctors until his TB. He smoked forty Woodbines a day and was smoking in hospital before he died of lung cancer. It was horrible, for Michael and I, to see him die like that. He was lying there, hardly able to breathe, listening to cassettes of The Furies and Foster and Allen (which made him cry every time he listened to them.) His favourites were "Maggie" and "When You Were Sweet Sixteen" and one or two others. Some must have been songs from his

Photos: Author's collection.

'Little Tonka', (middle of the back row) Fatfield School, circa 1922.

Billy Bankhead's Harmonica Band, 1934. From l. to r., back row standing: Larry
Greener, Gillie Scott, Billy Bankhead Snr., Billy Bankhead Jnr., Jack Aynsley.
Front row seated, from l.to r.: Bobby Thompson, Tommy Greener, Billy Aynsley.

Billy Aynsley. *Photo: D. Nicolson.*

Pat Healy. *Photo: D. Nicolson.*

Ed. Simmons.   *Photo: D. Nicolson.*

Lisle Willis.   *Photo: S Willis.*

Richard Kelly. Photo: D. Nicolson.

Joe Ging. Photo: D. Nicolson.

Bobby and Phyllis, 1959.   *Photo: Author's collection.*

Left to right: Michael and Keith Thompson.   *Photo: D.Nicolson.*

Paddy and Rosie Fox.   *Photo: D. Nicolson.*

vi

Danny La Rue. Photo: D. Nicolson.

Craig Douglas. Photo: D. Nicolson.

Brian Shelley.   *Photo: D. Nicolson.*

Father Cass.   *Photo: D. Nicolson.*

Left to right: Helen Russell and Corrinne Wilde.   *Photo: D. Nicolson.*

Left to right: Mark Lewis and Ronnie Vaughan.   *Photo: D. Nicolson.*

Homer Michaelides.   *Photo: D. Nicolson.*

To be completed only on club premises | NAME ....ヘﾞ??......ｦM...ﾗﾋﾞﾘﾐ...ﾐﾊ..........

Casino Royale Club

MEMBERSHIP REGISTER AND NOTICE OF
INTENT TO PARTICIPATE IN THE GAMING
in accordance with Section 12 of the Gaming Act 1968

The Secretary,
CASINO ROYALE CLUB,
Newcastle upon Tyne.

Dear Sir,
I hereby apply for membership of the Casino Royale Club and undertake that should I be elected by the committee I will accept and comply with the rules of the Club.
I appreciate that to comply with the requirements of the Gaming Act 1968 no member of the club or his quest may participate in gaming unless he has applied for membership in writing on the premises and that at least 48 hours have elapsed since that application or since becoming a member he has given notice in writing, on the club premises, to the Licence Holder or his representative, of his wish to participate in gaming. I hereby give notice to the Licence Holder or his representative on the club premises of my wish to participate in the gaming and I undertake to allow the necessary 48 hours to elapse before I or ny guests participate in any gaming at your club.
I confirm that I am at least eighteen years of age.

DATE 1C · 1C ˈ 1 ˈ   SIGNATURE

X

Paddy and Bobby, 'The Sunshine Boys'. *Photo: Author's collection.*

Stand............

.........and deliver!

'He's a freemason - puts fire places in for nowt'.

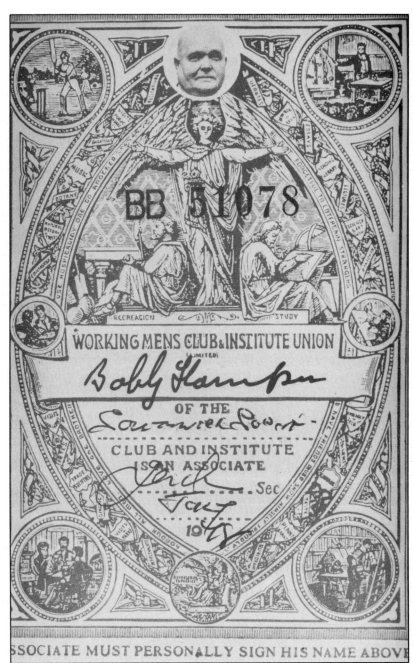

Bobby Thompson's last club card.

Mary Douglas and Bobby, 1980.   *Photo: D. Nicolson.*

Bobby and Cissie, 1983.   *Photo: Author's collection.*

Princes Gardens, Monkseaton.   Photo: D. Nicolson.

In
LOVING MEMORY
OF
A DEAR WIFE AND MOTHER
PHYLLIS THOMPSON
DIED 25TH APRIL 1967
AGED 56 YEARS.

LOVED AND REMEMBERED

Final resting place.   Photo: D. Nicolson.

childhood and he used to play one or two of them on his harmonica. He was lying in bed, unconscious, just a matter of an hour or two before he died, and we were playing the track of "When You Were Sweet Sixteen" to him. Although he couldn't see or hear us properly, he was actually crying - it was uncanny. The doctor said that his subconscious would actually be able to hear the music. We were chatting to him although he couldn't respond, as he was in a coma. But he was smiling and tried to put a hand to his face while "Maggie", another emotive song for him, was playing.

Moving forward to his funeral, there was a bouquet from a family called Larkin who were relatives of one of his sisters. That was the only tribute from his side. My dad came from a very big family and I think that he was the last surviving member. There were also a few wreaths and bouquets from my mother's side. The crowd at the cemetery was huge. I've never seen anything like it. As I drove up, every other person was somebody that I recognised : Mike Neville, George House, Bill Steel. Every comedian that you could think of from the North-East. Two of the Dallas Boys were there, Lonnie Donegan, Alan Snell, Alan Fox, Bobby Knoxall - absolutely everybody. It was quite moving to see all these people. For whatever reason they were there, they all paid their respects.

As dad was a Catholic, Michael and I wanted him to have a full Catholic burial in accordance with his expressed wishes to us. However, we had very little say in the matter as the decision to cremate him was made by his widow. The only way we could get around it was to buy the ashes afterwards for £25, get a nice box, and have them interred in our mother's grave. There were only four of us present for that private ceremony : Michael, myself, my girlfriend Elizabeth and Father Cass. My dad would never talk about things like illness, death or wills, due to his hypochondria. He believed that if you talked about a will then you were about to die. Then, lo and behold, when he died, a will surfaced which he had lodged with Lloyd's Bank. People will be surprised to learn that he left a considerable amount of property in his will.

This is the first time I've ever told anybody outside the people involved,

97

who are close family. He took very great care to see that property came into the hands of his grandchildren. However, because of his problem with the Official Receiver, these arrangements couldn't come to light. Had they done so, everything would have been taken away from him. That which we fight over now is obviously money. The reason I mention this is because my father was quite astute in many ways. Certainly, he was astute where money was concerned. He would claim to have nothing and he would let you think that he had nothing, but in fact he had plenty. 75% of everything was left to Michael and 25% to me, with £1,000 to go to Lottie's family. However, Cissie, Michael and I worked out a deal and agreed that everything should go three ways. In fairness, Cissie could, as his widow, have contested the will. The contents of the will confirmed what I'd always thought, that Michael was his favourite. However, it didn't really bother me, as Michael was still living at home and needed the money more than I did.

Discussing my dad like this has made me realise that he did everything his way. Moreover, he did it all with remarkable ease and made a living out of it. If I didn't pay my bills and went bankrupt, I'd be castigated. He didn't pay his bills, went bankrupt and was generally admired for it. You've got to take your hat off to him, he really did make an art of it. People think that he died with lots of debt. He actually didn't have any debt at all other than the tax-bill. Invariably, everything he bought was paid for by cash because that is how he operated. At this moment, there are plans for a headstone to be carved in the figure of my father. It is what he would have wanted, something to be on display for his public to see. He was always a showman, from the moment he stepped outside his home to the moment he got back.

We got off the train at Blackpool. The porter says: 'Carry your bag?'
Aa said: 'Let her walk.'

ED SIMMONS

I go back to 1947 with Bobby Thompson. It was when I was young, just after I came out of the Army. I used to drink in the Redheugh Pub, Gateshead, and it was there I first met him in company. After that, I used to see him all over, especially around Newcastle, with his mates. Then I took the taxi business on and he got me to drive him around from August, 1980. Between times, we had kept in touch when we met in different pubs. He was a bloody good sport - buy you a pint and give you a few Woodbines - he was good company and everybody enjoyed his crack. When I bought this taxi firm, some one called 'Wacky Jacky' used to run him around, and I took over from there. I drove him all over the place until he died and got to know him well. When you were driving, he would hardly speak to you, but when he did speak you got a good laugh. He would comment on things we saw in passing. He was very quick, very sharp to see the humour in anything.

My routine with him was to pick him up at his Princes Gardens house in Monkseaton, take him down to wherever he was working, which was all over the North-East, wait until the show ended, then fetch him back. If he was a bit short of money, he would go straight home, but he rarely did that. Normally, he would go straight to the Casino Royale Club, Newcastle and he would be there until two, three or four o'clock in the morning. I never waited for him there, just picked him up when he was ready to leave. Near the end, he started to get another taxi from there - I think it was the casino's staff taxi, but I'm not sure.

He had had his real hard days, working for coppers, and then he just broke away. It was Brian Shelley who fetched him away. He staked his reputation on Bobby to bring him back to fame. Bobby very seldom talked about his early life or childhood, he kept that to himself. He was a hell of a pigeon man. He never kept them himself, as far as I know, but if he went to a pigeon 'do' he was over the moon. The clubs were packed wherever he played in a mining area, it was always closed doors. Women liked him, especially the old-timers. He had a relation in Fatfield, Washington.. a nephew, called Larkin, I think. I was with him some years ago when we were doing a Washington club, the Stella Maris, and they met up there. Bobby said that it was the first time he had seen him for a long time.

As far as the people around him are concerned, I met most of them over the years. I knew his second wife, Phyllis, quite well.. she was a hard woman. They were well matched.. she could be coarse. At one time, if Bobby went into a club and couldn't get a seat he would walk out. He was prone to daft strokes like that. People knew that he had a daughter, Beatrice, from his first marriage, but Bobby never talked about her.

In my opinion, Bobby felt that Brian Shelley didn't treat him well towards the end, when arranging his monthly list of bookings. If an act didn't turn up, he would phone straightaway for Bob to go and we wouldn't know until we got there that someone else was supposed to be on. He wasn't giving him proper bookings, but I don't know why. Bobby always gave Brian his commission in cash. Then, Bobby joined Ronnie Vaughan of the Lewis Vaughan Agency, at Blyth. Ronnie gave him his week's bookings on a Monday morning and Bobby knew where he had to be each night. I think that Brian was trying to drop Bobby, as he was perhaps busy with other artists or business interests. But Bobby was as straight as a die... he was very straight forward, he kept nothing back. He did change his bookings, or do a 'double-up', and I agree that Shelley would have to dig him out on these occasions. No doubt, Brian has his own side of the story.

Bobby used to get a lot of nose-bleeds, and this time we were at Newton Aycliffe Legion Club. Bobby Webber went on the first half and Thompson went on the second. This night, we saw him start to change colour and we had to get him off the stage, he couldn't go on with his act. I took him home and sent for the doctor, but he was off for a week or a fortnight. That would be towards the end of 1987 or early in 1988. When he recovered, he went back to that club to do the booking as people would be upset at not seeing his act. They were all upset when he took bad and had all stood up. I used to tell him to keep off the mouth organ as I thought it caused the nose-bleeds and shortage of

100

breath. He did keep off playing it after that night and he was champion for a while. When he played it, his face used to go red.

He didn't do the Palladium show because he couldn't get his own lads on. They wanted nobody else but him from up here. I saw the playbill, but don't know what happened after that. When he couldn't get his acts on he said: 'That's it, I'm not going.' One of the acts he wanted on was Jason King. He wouldn't go into his reasons or likes and dislikes at all.

He liked horse-racing and the casino, to have a bet every day. Football interested him too. He used to go all over with his best pal, Paddy Fox, and his wife, Rosie. Paddy was the closest Bobby came to having a real mate. If there was anything wrong, Paddy was first there. Bobby used to take them on holiday to Blackpool with himself and Lottie Tate, his housekeeper for many years. I used to take them both all over. Bobby thought the world of Paddy.

I think he rented that house in Monkseaton because he had been brought up in hard times and enjoyed how he lived. He used to say that he had been on the bottom and was quite happy to stay on the bottom. He never complained if he was treated badly, but he wouldn't go back. Even if he was owed money, he wouldn't chase it. If he saw them, he would tell them it was about time that they paid up. He never fought with anybody. He had a few arguments, but no fighting. Some women used to chase him - they fancied him. In the early days, when I first knew him, he would knock drink back as fast as he could get it, usually Scotch or Brown Ale, but hardly bothered with spirits. When he went 'dry' I never saw him touch alcohol - tonic water was his drink - and you couldn't pay him to have a beer.

I remember taking him to see the tax-man - he wore no jewellery. He said: 'What makes you think aa've got any money - can you give me my fare home?' It didn't bother him at all. The tax-man tried to get him coming off stage with money at Dawdon Club, but the club wouldn't let him inside. If anyone official called to see him he would vanish, do the act and then vanish again. He wouldn't let anyone down outside of the

Inland Revenue. If he had a bill to pay, he would go straight home after the show - sometimes three times off the trot. When he had cleared the bill, he would go back to the casino. The Inland Revenue never turned up at the Casino Royale. Blackjack or Roulette were his pleasures. He knew the odds were against winning and had no illusions. The casino probably took two thirds of his earnings in the last six years of his life. He was bored and that was his excitement - sometimes he would pay them an afternoon visit as well as the regular evening one.

The people around him were given plenty. There were still large amounts of money coming in after his death and it annoyed me to read in the papers that he had left his family penniless, because he didn't. He paid for any debt and if anybody had outstanding HP on household items, then he wasn't responsible. At one time, he trusted no one but himself with the money. In later years, when his wife, Cissie, was with him, he told her to put the cash in her handbag. He was always paid on the night he did his turn, in cash. If the club had a cheque written out for him, they cashed it before he left. With clubs which had been tardy with paying him in the past, he insisted on cash before going on. Others paid him immediately afterwards, and many of them would show their faith by giving him cash, on their own initiative, before he went on.

When I was with him, his fees would be from £150, for a bad club on a week night, to between £180-£210. A really first-class club booking could pay him £250, and he loved the special event banquet bookings where he could command £500 for being the cabaret. As it was virtually all cash, I understand the VAT man didn't come into the picture. He was working-class and wanted to remain there and enjoy his pleasures. Money was only important to mark his work as an entertainer, not for material possessions - others around him were more interested in those.

He was a great man for the ladies and never had any difficulties - they loved and cherished him. The larger they were, the better he liked them, and I have driven him on a few afternoon 'hunts'. His fiancée, Mary Douglas, refused to move in with him, but he used to stay the weekend with her. His long-time passion was for a lovely lady called Mabel - it lasted for twenty years.

I remember the day he told me that he had hired a housekeeper, Cissie Palmer, and sent me over to collect her and take her to Princes Gardens. Bobby kept his subsequent marriage to Cissie very quiet, he would never discuss it. That was his private life and he could be very secretive. In the early years of their marriage, Cissie used to accompany him to his club bookings most nights and occasionally afterwards to the casino. Bobby loved playing to his audience and often invited her to join him on stage. However, I think that she got tired of hanging around in the clubs and in the last two years accompanied him very little.

He could be a jealous man and I am told that he once accused Cissie of having an affair with me. I thought about pulling him on the matter, but then saw the funny side of it and put it down to his sense of humour.

I have great memories of him and no regrets.

Aa went to the doctor. He said: 'Flu?'
Aa said: 'No, aa came here on my bike.'
He says: 'Can't find nothing wrong, it must be the drink.'
Aa says: 'Aa'll come back when ya're sober.'

RICHARD KELLY - 'MR KELLY'

I first came across Bobby when he came for an audition to the Newcastle studio of BBC Radio. This was more or less a matter of routine, but I used to have my contacts with concert parties and in the clubs and so on. It had been reported to me that this fellow was going around the clubs and that he might have some possibilities, so I arranged for him to come in. I don't think that it was he who applied for the audition.

Our practice, at the time, was to conduct these auditions in a listening room, where the curtains were drawn and we could not see the artist performing. A lot of comedians died a death because they were so visual. I'm talking now about the very early Fifties, 1951 - at the earliest. As we sat there listening to it, my assistant and I, we were convinced that there was not just one person in the studio but two, such was the authenticity of the wife's voice - particularly this screaming virago that he put on in those days. We had to part the curtains to make sure that he was the only one there. He was the only one, of course.

I fixed him up for an appearance, three weeks later, in 'Wot Cheor Geordie' (a show I was running at that time) at Cowpen, near Blyth. Let us be fair, it was a lucky break for me, I might add, as well as for him. I had some fairly good comedians, they were good lads, they worked at it, but I really needed someone with a bit of a spark. I thought that I had found it in Bobby. In fact, I was right. So, we were both lucky you might say, and he made his debut at Cowpen. We were fortunate in the fact that he was sharing the bill with Owen Brannigan, who was helpful to him on his first appearance as well as to the rest of us. It went like a bomb. He was the number two comedian at that time and top of the bill was Frank Burns. From that time, Frank Burns certainly had more than a slight resentment of Bobby, having been displaced as the number one comic.

I then put Bobby on every other week. The reason for this was that I thought a fortnightly appearance was the best that he could sustain, and I

104

think that I was right. After about half a dozen appearances, his material was not only exhausted - it was more than exhausted. The same stories coming over again and not dressed up all that differently either.

'Wot Cheor Geordie' played different venues all the time, this was the big thing about it. On my arrival there, the first thing that I did was take the programme out from the studio, where it had previously been, and around the mining villages - Cowpen being characteristic of the small towns of the North-East. Anyway, his material was running out, so I was faced with a problem. Here was a genuinely funny man and it was my job to find material for him, as I understood it. I tried a number of people and finally settled on a man called Lisle Willis. Every Monday, Lisle Willis and I would have a script conference. We would draft certain lines out for Bobby, incorporating characters and having certain set sequences - like the one, for instance, which would always start: 'The Chairman of the Shop Stewards comes in - her mother! I'm not kiddin' lads, there'll be a strike there soon.'

I thought Lisle Willis wrote very well for Bobby, in a way that was simple enough. Very difficult to get it straightforward so that Bobby was able to assimilate it. Willis continued to write for Bobby, with my co-operation. I made a few suggestions, but the bulk of the script was written by Willis. Bobby did perform an earlier script later on, but these situation scripts, written by Willis, were very successful. They were on a theme each week, and I think that Willis did very well by Bobby, but it has been my experience that dissension always seems to break out between comedians and writers. It certainly did with this writer, who was a mild enough mannered man, and bad feeling arose between him and Bobby, who alleged that Willis had said that he had been using part of his (Willis's) scripts in his club acts and on the stage. Willis pointed out that these scripts were commissioned for broadcasting only. He never got a penny out of Bobby, so I think that one might fairly say that Bobby was a bit tight-fisted - no matter how much money he was earning. It would have been quite easy for him to play along with this fellow, who wasn't making extraordinary demands, but no, he didn't want to part with the cash. Willis was paid on a contract basis by the BBC, through me, which was a rather different situation from the norm, but then we were dealing not with the West End of London, but with Newcastle and Tyneside, Wearside and Teesside.

Technically, there are no problems in radio. You just warn people not to get too close to the microphone, but apart from that you can forget about it. In many ways, it is easier in television, where they drape the microphone around your neck and there is no wiring. Bobby wasn't as well off as that, he had to play to a fixed microphone which could have inhibited him somewhat, but he managed to get over that all right.

However, Bobby did have trouble assimilating material - he was so slow. We would record a show on a Sunday, that was the routine. Then, from the previous week, there would be another situation script ready, and on Tuesday Bobby would come in and rehearse. And off and on he would rehearse on Tuesday, Wednesday, Thursday and Friday. He was in the studio with me quite a lot, interspersed with visits to the bar. It sounds as though I'm complaining, but I'm not. In fact, he had to have a drink and I enjoyed one too. The regular pub was the Burton House in Croft Street, Newcastle, next to the BBC. We would go over there and then we would come back and resume. He used to say that he had acquired his aptitude for timing from me. Well, timing certainly did come into it, but the main thing was getting him to learn a punch-line and relying upon him to get it right on the night, because one couldn't use these stock stories of his permanently. This was radio, they wanted something different every week. One example of his difficulties with a punch-line was the time we used an adaptation of a story about old Zacchariah, Bobby's daft old father-in-law, who was mortally ill in hospital.
Bobby was with him and saying: 'Oh, you'll soon be better.' Then, an aside: 'Well, you've got to cheer them up, haven't you?'
These callous asides used to appeal to these hard-boiled audiences in the pit villages.
Old Zaccariah then said: 'I only want to ask you one thing, Bobby. When I die, I want you to feel in my trouser pockets, at the bottom of the bed there, and you'll find two half crowns - with the rough edges. I want ye and Jonty and Charlie and Joe to carry me coffin. On the way

106

to the crem, you can put is doon, gan in, get yersel a pint each and leave me ootside - the way you've *always* done.'

Now this was it you see, we had to get this last line right.

Bobby said: 'And leave me outside the way you've always *done*'.

I said: 'No, Bobby, the way you've *always* done, not the way you've always *done.*'

He said: 'I've got it. Leave me outside, leave me outside... the way you've always done.'

'No! Bobby, No!' We used to go through this interminably. To spend an afternoon on a thing like this, or a lot worse, was nothing - it was not uncommon. At that time, we also had a number of his characters like the screaming wife, old Zaccariah, Herbert (the brother-in-law) etc. All of the characters were his creations, all except Herbert, who was based on a story he told (not one we could use.) They were all his, he came with them. It was our job to build these characters up in order to eke out the material he had already brought along. Sadly, at the time of his greatest glory, all of these characters, who really established him, were abandoned.

We may have developed the characters, but nobody created Bobby Thompson, he was his own man. He was immensely popular, like no other comedian in the North-East has been since the time of Jimmy Learmouth - which was before my time. The novelist, J.B. Priestley, reckoned that Jimmy Learmouth was the funniest man that he had ever seen in his life, but I think that Priestley would have changed his mind if he had seen Bobby. I think that Bobby's great strength was that however much he disparaged his own kind, kidded them along, and even insulted them, they loved him because they knew that he was one of them. He knew all of their weaknesses and he was part of their community. In doing so, he displayed all of his own weaknesses in the process - and outside of the process too. He was not separate from the people he was performing for. He was one of them. You always felt with the other comedians, good though they might be, that they were standing outside of it all, but not so with Bobby. He seemed to project the anxieties, the minor miseries, the preoccupations, the habits, the money problems, the living problems, and he used to do all this with a tremendous knack of making it all seem acceptable and funny. In other words, Bobby Thompson was a real comedian, he wasn't a fictitious, artificial comedian. I used to go and see him in the clubs when we worked together.

You ask me how much of his success at that time was due to the scripts. Well, I don't think that Lisle Willis, who is dead now, would have claimed that he either originated or altered the essence of Bobby Thompson. He provided a means whereby this extraordinary comic talent could be deployed, particularly in radio, to longer and better advantage. For my part, I had rehearsed him. I had to teach him how to hold back a punch-line, how to deliver a punch-line. In my view, this was no more than common sense on my part, but you were dealing with a man who was having trouble memorising the thing in the first place. I had to make allowances for the fact that he had difficulty memorising - and still more did he have difficulty working from a script. He couldn't memorise the whole script, he had to have it on a stand in front of him. It wasn't like his own parrot act, which was written in an illiterate hand on the back of an envelope - if he had it at all. He didn't find this easy, but it was the price he had to pay for continuous appearance on radio in a weekly show, and this went on for years.

Sometimes, he didn't turn up on time and you had to put the fear of God into him. I think that he once said there were only three people he was ever afraid of: his wife, the colliery manager and me - in that order. You had to threaten him for his own good. There was trouble with the drink and I had to threaten him about that too. His wife, Phyllis, was my ally in this. She would tip me off about what he was getting up to, and in addition to her giving him a rollicking, he got one from me as well. This more or less kept him - I won't say on the straight and narrow, it was never that - in check. There were times when we had to sober him up slightly. Obviously, drink was a problem. I would say that the drink was a problem because he was feeling a lot of pressure. Bobby was a cunning man rather than a clever or intelligent one. He had great trouble assimilating this material for a weekly performance, so he sought relief from the tension in drinking. It was quite natural, but of course it had to be avoided in excess, as some people would call it. Personally, I think you either drink or you don't. I don't agree with the theory of drinking to excess. Some people can't help it.

Bobby was driven by the money, the fame and the prestige. We are talking about the early Fifties, and the prestige of appearing on a BBC Radio show was fantastic. It was fantastic for me - and I was only the producer. He was the star. Of course, what he should have done, had he had more foresight, was to have behaved himself and turned up for engagements when he had promised to do so. Instead, he jettisoned everything cynically if he was offered a quid or two more somewhere else. That was his undoing in the first place. Had he been a more conventional character he would have done much better, but then that is the way he was. I never contemplated managing him. I wouldn't have done that, I had no reason to do so either. I was all right at the BBC and had an interesting job. Even if he had been acclaimed nationally, I still wouldn't have managed him. I wouldn't have wanted that, thank you very much.

We dropped the title 'Wot Cheor Geordie' for a while and I put Bobby on alone with 'Bob's Your Uncle'. Due to difficulties in obtaining the material and getting him to assimilate it, that format was impossible to sustain, and so we went back to the act type of show as 'Wot Cheor Geordie' was called.

This arrangement went on until he went to Tyne Tees Television around 1959. I had decided that we had had enough of light entertainment acts and that there was little future for scripted shows (on radio, anyway) and that if I was to stay in radio, either willingly or unwillingly, I had to find some other kind of programme that promised more. It was at this point that I switched from light entertainment into news and topicality. Bobby went to Tyne Tees TV, partly because of this change, I think, but principally - you need seek no further than this - he went to Tyne Tees because it was television and this was the mass media now, not radio. Things had changed in those ten years. He was right to go to television, absolutely right. I didn't begrudge him it. I wished him good luck.

The tragedy was that he went to join a bunch of people who, I believe, were totally unable, through inexperience or whatever, to present him properly. They didn't seem to understand Bobby Thompson or his humour. When he arrived at Tyne Tees to appear in this jimcrack situation comedy, they would probably say: 'Well, where's your script? Get on with your act. This is what we pay you for - £200 a throw.' Bobby was a bit bemused by this. At the BBC, the producer, Mr Kelly, no less, provided him with a script and coached him as to how to do it. He didn't get that at Tyne Tees for the money they were paying him, which was more than he was getting at the BBC. He was probably getting £50 or so a week on radio, I don't really remember. It wasn't the money you got at the BBC in the radio days, it was the prestige and Bobby was astute enough to realise this. Certainly, he never argued over money. You went out and got your money by topping the bill elsewhere to people who had never seen you. 'Bobby Thompson in the Flesh', 'Bobby Thompson In Person'. That was how you made your money. It was a fair enough arrangement in many ways. You appeared on the BBC, but made your fortune elsewhere - if you were all that good. Anyway, from that time on, it was many years before I saw him again. He never discussed his problems with me, either about Tyne Tees or when he was down after that. I lost total contact with him during those years and during his resurgence many, many years later. He suffered some dreadful deprivations:- the death of his wife, the dole, appearing in 'Go As You Pleases' in workingmen's clubs, hospitalisation and the threat that drink would kill him if he didn't stop. I wasn't with him through any of that. I give him full credit for pulling himself up again because he did it without the benefit of the radio and television. I think it was a remarkable revival, and all credit to him for achieving it.

My relationship with Bobby Thompson was a professional relationship tinged with a sort of camaraderie, but it wasn't a personal relationship in that we didn't frequent each other's homes or that sort of thing. He did discuss how he felt about things professionally, but it was mostly to say how well he was getting on and what he was earning in the clubs and theatres. His attitude towards other comedians was a bit patronising and I never saw him doubt himself. If he had any self-doubts, he was clever enough to conceal them. Without having any sort of education, Bobby was still a bit too clever for his own good. The rest of the cast who did the shows with us seemed to regard him as a bit of an oddity more than anything else. He enjoyed being the centre of attention, which he was, quite rightly, and in the public house after a show he would be getting the pints in. But I learnt very quickly that he got that first round paid for by prior arrangement with the landlord. It didn't come out of his own pocket, and others would get their round in afterwards. But he wasn't hoity-toity. For instance, he didn't treat the commissionaires with disdain. I suppose, in a sense, he would be more at home with commissionaires than he would be with these arty crafty musicians, singers and what have you, but he didn't spend his money on other people. I don't know whether I really should say this, but I had a secretary who was a very hard working girl and she did a lot for Bobby on the side. He used to come in and say: 'Oh, Doreen has done this, that or the other on the side for me, I'll get her a bottle of gin.' And then a week later he would say: 'Oh, Doreen has done this, that or the other. She helped me work this out on a contract... I'll get a half a bottle of gin for her.' I noticed that the gift had dropped by this time. This went on week after week and I said: 'Look, it is no business of mine, either you buy her a bottle of gin or you don't buy her a bottle of gin, but for God's sake stop talking about it!' He never did buy the gin.

His personal quirks didn't worry me. What I was concerned about was getting that final punch-line of the show over. There was this big moment - it was the biggest moment, I think, in the whole of my experience of light entertainment and 'Wot Cheor Geordie' in particular. I'll never forget it. This was at Ferryhill, the Miners' Welfare Hall - the year would be 1951/52, when the Government seemed to be changing every year and the big issue was the Health Service - free specs, free teeth, free wigs, and all that sort of thing. There was tremendous Conservative opposition to all this. Bobby told this story - by the way I'm not sure it wasn't a Willis story dressed up for him, but I could be wrong about that. The scene is the club - where else? The wireless is on and the election results are just coming in thick and fast. Bobby's father-in-law, old Zachariah, is sitting there with his pint of Fed

(Federation Ale) in front of him, reading the sporting pages and peering through his glasses. He has one pint after another, and the wireless is droning on... 'Conservative gain, Conservative gain... Conservative gain'. Old Zacha dozes off, and then at three o'clock the steward comes around: 'Howwaay lads, lets ha' your glasses.' At this old Zacha wakes up with a start and says: 'Ye bugger, are the Tories back already?'

You should have heard it at Ferryhill - I have never heard anything like it in my life. They roared with laughter, they clapped, somebody had a church bell and started ringing it, they started whistling. Bobby was on the stage and he was dancing around, milking them for all he was worth. At the time (and this was a long time ago), the show was recorded not on tape, but on disc in Manchester, and of course you had to get the timing of the half hour absolutely right. This was going on and on and he wouldn't let go of them. I was furiously signalling the band to go straight into the play-off before time. There was another act to follow to finish the half hour. That was, I think, one of his big moments. It was certainly one of mine. I thought that was one of the great comic moments of radio - 'Ye bugger, are the Tories back already?' Anybody would have got a high out of that, whether you described yourself as a comedian or not. If you could put a story like that across and get a reaction of that kind, why it was better than Churchill or Hitler or anybody. They never got such a ready response as that.

There were certain superficial resemblances to other comedy actors, but I don't think the resemblances did him any good and I told him to steer clear of them. He had obviously studied Jimmy James, from whom he got the cigarette routine, and I tried to keep him off this style. Having said so much about my time with him in the early days, I would like to say, in fairness, that when I saw his revival, in particular the two solo performances he gave for Tyne Tees TV, I was impressed. I don't think that they were up there with the best of his earlier performances, simply because the characters were missing (he reckoned that he couldn't do the wife's voice any more, for instance, because it was too much of a strain for him) and some of the material - even a lot of the one-liners - didn't suit the style I had known. Nevertheless, I thought that he had got some good material. I don't know where he got it from, and I don't believe it was simply people walking through his house or sending jokes on the back of an envelope. I think he must have had somebody working with him who never received any credit. That would be in line with his quarrels with the scriptwriter in my time.

When we met up again, after his successful comeback, he was always very friendly with me and kind in the things that he said about our time together on radio. At his invitation, my wife and I attended some of his performances and we were always 'properly looked after', as he would say. I enjoyed all his live performances on television. However, I think he made one or two mistakes. For instance, part of his Army sketch involved real characters, the Prime Minister, Neville Chamberlain, ringing him up and saying: 'Eeh, Bobby, I'm in an awful fix' etc. There was a certain humour about it, but it didn't have that close contact with reality. It wasn't the same as the story about debt: 'There's plenty of money around here, look at the amount we owe.' It wasn't so close - these impersonations of famous characters were works of imagination, not realism. They wouldn't have worked without the costume. I must say, although I do not like the rest of the act, the first appearance is hilarious when he comes on in this bedraggled battledress. Everybody bursts into laughter and he looks at them sternly, with his one eye, and says: 'You didn't laugh when aa was fighting for ya.' I think that is a great line, an absolutely great line. The idea of the fate of the country, and its people, depending on this greasy, filthy looking creature - I like that. Nothing to do with me, I didn't rehearse him with that, nor did I write it, nor did any writer of mine write it, but all credit to whoever thought that one up, it was really good.

Bobby definitely had the costume of cap, long jersey and baggy trousers in the Fifties, although, to the best of my recollection, he didn't wear the Little Waster outfit at his first appearance for me and the BBC at Cowpen. When he appeared in this raggy, Charlie Chaplin type, gear, he would always wear an extremely expensive wool pullover underneath. On his hands, he wore jewellery, as much as to say, I am only acting this, I've made it really - I'm worth a bob or two now.

Regarding Phyllis's influence, she did her best. Of course, I was not to know what was hers and what was his of the material. She wasn't interfering, she was very co-operative was Phyllis. 'A face like an unmade bed' - as Albert Burdon described her rather unkindly.

We tried to get him off the maudlin songs, but we did try to get him to do a take-off of Josef Locke in a rather fruity voice: 'Here they go, what a show, those guardsmen...' etc. Bobby's posh accent was absolutely excruciating - I don't think he always knew how dreadful it was. We put in the odd pop song that we thought he could take the mickey out of - like "Am I a Toy, or Am I a Treasure?" The thing is, he wasn't playing in time with the band. He would get a run in from them and I had to be there to give him the cue. We did it at rehearsal with the pianist, but he always missed it. I thought that this was just adding another headache to it. I couldn't cope with this as well, so we didn't do many of them. He took himself seriously as a singer. What I wanted him to do was take the mickey out of Josef Locke, which wasn't difficult, and I wanted him to take these amorous pop songs and make them funny with this absurd voice. I wanted it to be a spectacle as well as sound funny. But he would always get mixed up somewhere and it would come out a shambles. We used to re-record to get it right after the audience had gone, and somehow or other get the audience in by cutting the tape. It was always in front of a live audience. Audience reaction was never fed in. He abandoned the suit quite early on with us, at our suggestion, when we told him to do the act in the clothes he would normally wear.

I did a piece about him for The Observer Magazine. As soon as he saw it on the Sunday morning, he sent the lad out to buy the whole lot up from newsagents and ended up with a great big pile of Observers. He was proud at having made a national newspaper, a respectable one too. He didn't systematically go out of his way to get publicity.

In my opinion, he wasn't capable of national stardom. I don't think that he had the stamina. This was nothing to do with his merits as a comedian, but I just don't think that he had the will and so on. Greedy though he was, he was too feckless rather than easy going. I think he was probably right to have pulled out of the Palladium performance because the Geordie accent is more difficult for people to understand than other regional dialects. On the other hand, he was accepted all over the North and people used to write in and say how much they loved 'Wot Cheor Geordie' - even though they didn't understand a word of it! I'll never understand that - how can you enjoy anything when you can't understand a word of it. But the letters used to come in shoals from Lincolnshire, Derbyshire and all over the place. I just can't imagine him going down well in the Home Counties, and can't imagine him in the West Country. In the Midlands, he would have probably gone down all right.

Regionally, he could have done more for himself and better managed his affairs. It is a funny sort of career when you get virtually to the top, then plunge again through drink and greed and what have you, then become a reformed character and get up to the top again. Looking back, you can say that with a bit of thought he might have avoided that dip. Certainly he made mistakes, but he came back - largely with a lot of help from his manager, Brian Shelley. I think you have to give credit there, but largely it was due to his own efforts.

Bobby could read, in the sense that he wasn't illiterate, but he wouldn't read very much. He'd read one of the tabloids, the headlines and so on - a bit of a story. But he couldn't spell, I can tell you that - he kept story cues on the back of envelopes, the spelling was something incredible, but it didn't matter. The social aspects of success didn't bother him and he never bought his home in Monkseaton - it suited him. Why should he put all this money down for a mortgage, if he was paying something like 27/6d rent?

In my time with him, I never saw him really angry or spoiling for a fight - never. Physically, he wasn't in a position to do so, was he? 'Six-and-a-half stone wet through', as he used to describe himself. He was never child-like to work with either, he was an ordinary chap with an eye on the main chance. He didn't really have any strong feelings on anything socially or politically, but the story that I told you about the reaction to the election results was because he knew people were talking and thinking about that. It wasn't that he had any particular attitude. He had no illusions about the people that he lived among. I think that he would have laughed at you if you had started talking about this sort of salt of the earth rubbish, but I am not saying that he was cynical.

I never knew anything about his childhood - the earliest I heard about him was when he was briefly called up into the army, in the Border Regiment. How on earth he was called up to the Border Regiment, God only knows. He couldn't have been of much use to them. Anyway, he became a runner and, still with an eye on the main chance, he used to make barter arrangements for the Captain, whose runner he was. He had a bicycle for this and would swap bottles of gin for loaves of bread and he is very funny when he relates these stories. He had total recall. Bobby could have been a great story teller and conversationalist, never mind a professional entertainer. He could have been good company, but he always had this feeling that he had to watch what he said and say the right thing to people who had any influence.

Every time aa look at her, aa appreciate mercy killing.

Last week, we weren't speakin'. Last Tuesday neet, aa was talkin' to mesel an' aa'll tell ye what aa said. Aa says: Bobby, why divven't ye get a shave an' gan out an' get drunk an' come in, get thee supper an' gan to bed, get up an' get thee breakfast, an' gan out, come in, get thee dinner an' gan to bed. An' aa didn't contradict mesel.

JOE GING - 'CHISLETT, LAD'

I first came across him when I used to listen to this marvellous radio programme called 'Wot Cheor Geordie' which featured local comedians including Bobby. At the time, Dickie Irwin was 'King Dick' as the local big comedian and Bobby came along and put his nose out of joint. I first met him in the 1950s when I worked with a friend of mine. We used to do satirical stuff and of course it was 'ower their heeds' in those days. However, Dick (Kelly) thought he might be able to use us and I did a warm-up for one of the 'Wot Cheor Geordie' shows in 1955.

Bobby saw me as I came off and walked over to give me some encouragement. The conversation went along the following lines.

'That wasn't bad.'

'Oh, thanks very much.'

'Where does thou work?'

'Newcastle.'

'Well, there's not enough work in Newcastle.'

'I just do this as a hobby.'

'As a what?'

'I do this for fun.'

'Right, lad, ne body does this for fun.'

That was the first time I met him, and after that my partner and I used to do the introductions to the Bobby Thompson programme. We did 'Wot Cheor Geordie' for the whole series.

During one of those series, or it might have been earlier, Dick Kelly used to send the full scripts out to everyone. On one occasion, Dickie Irwin was in the bar, before the show, reading some of Bobby's material and saying: 'Now, isn't this aaful? Now, isn't this aaful?' There was a hell of a big row and Dick Kelly decided, quite rightly, that from then on he'd only top and tail a person's act and wouldn't send out the full script. That is really when I first realised the animosity that Dickie Irwin had toward Bobby Thompson, although Bobby felt no resentment in return - he couldn't be bothered. However, there was this rivalry between them which Bobby only inadvertently began because he was so good. But Dickie was jealous, he was being challenged and it was the old cock and the young cock I suppose. After the script row, I have a feeling that they were kept apart, because Dick didn't want any trouble. Dickie Irwin was very clever, an intellectual but didn't know it, but also an awkward and difficult man. So, Bobby eventually did his own series, 'Bob's Your Uncle'.

At the end of one of the series, recorded at the Priory Theatre, Whitley Bay, we were all invited, by Bobby, across to the Avenue pub on the front. By this time, my friend, Coulson Scott, and I had got to know Bobby quite well and were aware that he was a bit of a tight-arse. So, it came as no surprise to us when we discovered later on that Bobby had got a back-hander from the manager to bring us in, but we weren't bothered. The Barry Sisters did an act, we all got up and did something, just for fun and relaxation after the show. The finish of it was when Phyllis, Bobby's wife, got up and recited an old poem. It was about going to heaven and not being allowed in by St Peter who asked: 'What have you done to deserve coming into heaven?' and she said: 'I was married to Bobby Thompson,' so she was allowed straight in. She did it very well and Coulson thought that this was his chance to make peace with Phyllis, who didn't like him because she thought that he was looking down his nose at her. He wasn't, he was and is a very kind man. Coulson went across to her and his story is as follows.
'Hello, Phyllis, congratulations.'
'Whaa aboot?'
'About your poem.'
'Oh,' she said: 'I thowt ye were congratulatin' is because Bobby's ganna be a fatha.'
'All the more reason to congratulate you.'
'Ye divvent understand, I'm not the mother.'
That was in 1955 and I would imagine that there are possibilities of it being true. After that, Bobby was around and about broadcasting very regularly with Dick Kelly.

I remember seeing Dick in 1959. Tyne Tees Television was just opening and Dick said: 'They've offered Bobby the chance to go on television and I've tried to persuade him not to do it.' The reason was that Bobby was not tele-visual and he was difficult in so far as he wasn't really an educated man. If I can just digress a moment, perhaps I can illustrate what I mean. We were rehearsing one day and he had to say the words 'coffee permutator' and we all laughed. Bobby looked surprised and said: 'I don't know why you are all laughing, we've got a coffee permutator at yem.' Now, whether he was pulling our legs I don't know, you could never be quite sure with Bobby which way it was going, but that did actually happen with him and there were other similar instances.

Dick Kelly was genuinely concerned. He said: 'All right, I have lost him, but it doesn't matter anyway. That kind of programme will no longer do because of television and we are doing other things.' (He went onto something called 'Vox Pop', which he developed, interviewing in the streets. It was a good idea.) Dick told me: 'I just don't want Bobby to be destroyed.'

Bobby went to Tyne Tees to do his own series, 'The Bobby Thompson Show'. I believe the first programme attracted the biggest viewing audience they ever had and the last one received the lowest. At this time, there were people at Tyne Tees called the One O'clock Show Gang who were from the variety theatre, which was dying when Tyne Tees opened. The gang included competent performers like Terry O'Neill, Peggy Haig, Jack Haig and Len Marten, the scriptwriter from Charlie Chester's programme. Now, Len was a very good scriptwriter, a competent performer and not a bad stand-up comic. Anyway, they decided that some of these artists were going to play the parts of Bobby Thompson's imaginary radio family, which never works. It's like when you try to do the Goons as a cartoon - it doesn't work as you have got your own mental image. Len Marten playing Herbert (Bobby's effeminate brother-in-law) wasn't Herbert. Similarly, although Phyllis played the part of his wife, she wasn't an actress and she was uneasy with it. Certainly, this first experience of television was a disastrous one for Bobby Thompson.

After Tyne Tees, Bobby was really struggling, rapidly went downhill and became unreliable. One of the gags in the clubs was when people would walk on the stage and announce an impersonation of Bobby Thompson. They would wait a while and then say: 'The Little Waster hasn't turned up again!' This was accepted as a joke in the clubs as they knew he was very, very unreliable. At this time, he needed the stern benevolence of Dick Kelly. Bobby appreciated that handling and always called him Mr Kelly. He readily acknowledged that he owed everything to the man. In my opinion, he did. I don't think he would ever have taken off in the first place without Dick recognising that, in this raw material, here was a natural, wonderful, outstanding comedian. Dick saw all this, worked with Bobby and worked very hard. The other comedians around at the time in the series were competent comedians, but not outstanding. They just didn't have that little touch which Bobby had. When he left the ken of Dick, he disappeared for quite a while and I think this Tyne Tees programme knocked his confidence. It would certainly have knocked mine. I don't know how they got through the whole thing. There were all sorts of stories, but I wasn't in there so I don't know.

In 1962, they re-opened Balmbra's Music Hall in Newcastle's Cloth Market. There were three of us doing the chairing there. There was Arthur Clarence, who came from a long line of music hall performers, Dickie Irwin and myself. Dickie Irwin was a very competent chairman, probably the best of the three of us. I was doing a kind of Leonard Sachs, to be different from the other two. We had two nights a week each. Arthur kept the Friday and Saturday, I was Wednesday and Thursday and Dickie had Monday and Tuesday (he had bookings the rest of the week and Monday and Tuesday were his quiet nights.)

Bobby rang me up at home one night and said: 'Hoo, Chislett, lad, will thou do Monday and Tuesday at Balmbras?' I said: 'I'm sorry Bobby, I do Wednesday and Thursday.' He said: 'I know, but you know what it is like - thon Dickie Irwin will kill my act.' This was true. Dickie, if he didn't like somebody (or if it was a comedian who was good), would do a twenty-minute spot himself, before they went on, which meant that the person's act would be ruined. Anyway, I asked Dickie if I could do the Monday and Tuesday and we swapped. I can't remember whether or not I made an excuse. On the night, I just gave Bobby a normal, proper introduction. As it happened, I liked the man, liked his act and the way he did things. I thought he was very funny. I had nothing to do with putting the shows on, I just did my little bits. A man called Benny Cunningham put the shows on and Betty Drew produced them. Bobby went down very well on both nights and he bought me a double whisky on the Tuesday - which was like a hundred quid from anybody else. He said: 'Now, thon Dickie Irwin can do what he likes, Chislett, lad. I've had agents in and I've got some bookings, and thou's responsible 'cos thou's helped me. I'll not forget it.' As far as I was concerned, his success had nowt to do with me, the lad was a good comedian and all I did was my job.

Perhaps I should explain that he called me Chislett because I was working as Chislett Ging. There was already a comedian called Joe King, so they wouldn't let me use my own name of Joe Ging. My middle name is Chislett, so I became Chislett Ging. Coulson also had to change his name (from Coulson to Gilbert) because Dick Kelly said it was too unusual. So I could use Chislett Ging, but he couldn't use Coulson Scott, it was strange.

Balmbra's was quite a prestigious place and Bobby must have approached Benny Cunningham for a spot on the show. There was certainly no money in it. I remember Dickie Irwin saying that it cost him money to work there. I asked him how he worked that out and he said that by the time he had his beer he was out of pocket. It was just fun and that's why I used to do it. Funnily enough, Dickie Irwin took no pleasure in Bobby's demise. When people are down, people like Dick Irwin will help them. It is only when they are going up that they want to pull them back to their level. That's human nature.

After his appearance at Balmbra's, I didn't see much of Bobby, but Harry Green, who married June of the Barry Sisters and was Richard Kelly's studio manager, used to collect Bobby Thompson stories and here are three that he told me.

They were performing one of the programmes in Stockton and they arrived at this hotel for an evening meal. Bobby put on what he called his ready-money voice and went up to the reception desk.

'Could I see the menu?' he asked in this posh voice.

The woman said: 'I'm sorry, the chef hasn't come in yet.'

'Hasn't come in yet?' said Bobby imperiously: 'It's now seven o'clock and you start serving at seven-thirty. It must be chips!'

When Bobby was playing Buttons in 'Cinderella' during the 1959/60 panto season at Newcastle Empire Theatre, Harry asked how the show was doing. Bobby told him that there were only two empty seats in the place - one in the Ladies and one in the Gents.

One Christmas, he gave Harry a cigarette lighter, and Harry, being very touched, said: 'Thank you very much.' Bobby said: 'Oh, no, I got a whole load of them for nowt.'

So, he became a byword in the area and he eventually came back again and became very well known. Occasionally, I used to see him if I was doing a music hall somewhere. I liked sitting on the stage when Bobby was on because you could listen to him again and again and still laugh. He came across during the laughter of one of the shows when I was sitting on the stage and said: 'Hoo, Chislett, thou's still laughin' and thou's heard them all.' But he couldn't understand why I had that regard for him as a very funny man.

It is fascinating with comedians. There are these natural comedians, who if they start to analyse what they've got it disappears. I imagine Bobby kept off that side of things. The women seemed to go for this funny little man. Another example of that was with that amazing artist, Little Tich. When they wanted certain women out of the country (the mistresses of Edward VII), they would ask him to perform in Paris, knowing that these women would follow him there. There is quite a resemblance between Little Tich, Bobby Thompson and the greatest of them all, Dan Leno. They have all got this characteristic little face, the thin comedian's face and the sad, sad eyes. That is always the sign of a good comedian, the sad eyes, they do help. I think Bobby liked women. After all, he would be a very strange man if he didn't, but he never showed it when I was around.

One of his gags was that he worked the Grand Theatre, Byker and then it closed, and he worked a place in Workington and it closed. He used to say: 'I've cleared mair theatres than anybody else aa knaa.' What used to happen was that he would be the last gasp. They would get Bobby in to try to keep the place going. When he couldn't keep it going, it would close. He had the Merry Magpies at the Grand for a long run and his leading lady was Edna Dean, who still works the clubs.

Phyllis was involved quite a lot with Bobby's career. I was in to see Dick Kelly one day and he told me that they had just re-edited the programme from the previous night - it was one of the 'Bob's Your Uncle' shows. Bobby had kept mentioning that he was going to have this beer, because it was a *man's* beer. Now, at that time Watney Mann wasn't known up here, as it was one of the London breweries. Phyllis came into the BBC and told them that Bobby had got a back-hander for mentioning Mann's beer on the programme, so they had to re-edit it. Like everybody else, Dick didn't know about this Mann's beer, which apparently they were just hoping to bring into the North-East at the time. This would be in the mid-Fifties. Bobby was foolish enough to think that he could get away with something like that, but Phyllis realised that it was a stupid thing to do and could just about finish him with Dick Kelly. Dick is one of these people who is very very straight and would never deviate in any way whatsoever. At that time, the BBC was also extremely strict, nothing like that was mentioned at all, whereas today anything seems to go.

How Herbert, the effeminate character, got into the act was that Bobby was talking to Dick in a pub one night and told him this story. The Salvation Army was playing at the corner of the street and the lassie gans roond with the tambourine. This fella puts a ten bob note in and she says: 'Eeh, that's very kind of you, what hymn would you like?' The fella replies: 'Him with the big drum.' Dick told him that he could use the character (but not the gag) and that's how Herbert began. That story came from Bobby Thompson himself.

A lovely Roy Hudd story. Roy Hudd had Bobby on his programme, called 'Halls of Fame', at Sunderland Empire. I worked with Roy on the script. He told me that he walked in and saw this little fella with a jersey on, and thought he was one of the stage hands. He didn't realise it was Bobby, but said that when he heard him perform he had never known any timing like it. It was just superb, as was his rapport with the audience which was so admirable. I phoned Roy a couple of years later. It was when Rock Hudson was dying of AIDS and there is this classic story of Bobby's, that you might have heard, where he says: 'For years I wanted to look like Rock Hudson, and now he looks like me.' Of course, as you will appreciate, all pros have a very cruel sense of humour and Roy Hudd said that the joke went like a bomb at the Water Rats. Bobby didn't tell the joke, Roy Hudd quoted it at the Water Rats about Bobby. A lot of them knew Bobby, about his reputation and how highly he was regarded in the North-East. It is quite amazing, in my opinion, how he became lauded well after his best years - which were those with Richard Kelly and the 'Wot Cheor Geordie Show'. I could compare him to the Thirties comedian, Sandy Powell, who was a competent comedian and made one or two films, but if you live long enough you become a cult figure in this business. It is not a business where people are renowned for longevity, I suppose. Somebody like Sandy Powell could get by with two very funny acts - the conjurer and the ventriloquist - and they become cult acts, but in fact he would never have been remembered if he hadn't lived so long.

Some of the well loved characters on screen are very unpleasant people in private life. With Bobby, I was never near enough to him to find out. We passed the time of day when we were together, but that was about all. I don't even know whether he was a sociable man, I wouldn't have thought so. Rather, a very secretive man with few close friends.

One of the BBC producers, Roger Burgess, did a programme about a woman who used to sing in clubs, before the war, in a baritone voice. They got Bobby on because he knew her. The programme was done about 1980 or '81 and I went along just to help Roger. I saw Paddy Fox, Bobby's friend, who never spoke all night, just carried gear in and out.

The last time I saw Bobby was when Phil Penfold, of the Evening Chronicle, interviewed him on Radio Newcastle and we had a little chat in the bar afterwards. It was extremely pleasant and he seemed in very good spirits. It was just after he'd had this dreadful trouble with the tax-man and the interview was a good one. I don't think he was a worrier, but I could be wrong. I just think he had such a terrible childhood that anything in comparison was canny. Like myself, he was one of a large family. By today's standards we were deprived, but neebody telt wi' so we were happy.

Bobby was a natural at acting and his voices were excellent. He could do any amount of different voices for different characters and get that lovely shaded nuance. He had a very good novelty act which I only saw him do when he was touring big theatres - that was the one where he stood behind a screen on stage and, with a back projection light, did his Charleston dance act. It was quite an amazing sight. He was an extremely agile person and apparently had been a champion dancer in his younger days in the Twenties. He did this fantastic act which you did not associate with Bobby Thompson, who you would always think of as a radio comedian and nothing else. Picked up and trained at the right time, I reckon that he could have done all sorts of things, despite the accent, because he could do it physically. He could have dropped the accent if he had wanted to, but maybe he felt safer in the North-East. There is the classic story of him when he was being interviewed on radio and the interviewer asked: 'How far can you perform from Newcastle?' and Bobby replied: 'Aboot thirty mile.' The interviewer then said: 'In view of your record coming out, how far can you perform now?' and he replied: 'Aboot another half mile.' He knew that he could only go so far with his act.

I have done quite a lot of research on the Italian clowns, the Commedia dell'Arte, the amoral character of Arlequino or Harlequin. To me, Bobby Thompson was the epitome of that character and, picked up at the right time, he could have been a most wonderful Arlequino. This man got into all sorts of mischief - just for the sake of sweet devilment - and it was mainly physical because the Italian clowns didn't talk a lot. I don't compare his style with Chaplin, because Charlie went out of his way to make everybody feel sorry for him, to love him, whereas Bobby never did that.

THE YOUNG NURSE - MRS M M STARBUCK

I was a final-year student nurse in the Fifties and one day, when I was in charge of the Casualty Department, at the Sunderland Royal Infirmary, I heard a lot of talking coming from the waiting room. I opened the clinic door, to see what was going on, and was amazed to see all the waiting patients standing around in a circle, cackling with laughter. My first thought was that if I didn't get this noise sorted out, Matron would be down on me like a ton of bricks and I would receive another black mark. As I approached this circle of patients, I noticed someone standing in the middle. Who was it? 'Wor Bobby', who was appearing at Sunderland Empire at the time (1954-1955.)

Although delighted that he was keeping the patients occupied happily, I was terrified in case Matron should pounce! I asked him to come through to see the doctor. He said: 'Eeh, pet, it's not my turn yet.' I told him the other patients wouldn't mind and rushed him through into the clinic. He had cut his thumb on a can opener, and it was bleeding heavily and needed stitches. He'd wrapped it up in an old cloth.

More hilarity followed. Bobby was in his trade mark clothes and when the casualty officer, who was broad Irish, came to look at his thumb, he raised his eyebrows at the way Bobby was dressed. Bobby said not a word, but gave the doctor one of his comical looks. Now, you must bear in mind that this doctor had never heard of 'Wor Bobby', so he asked the usual question. 'How did you do this exactly?' Bobby looked at me and I realised he couldn't understand the broad Irish accent, plus the doctor was not a man who had a sense of humour! He was not amused at Bobby's cheeky expression. Well, I knew that the doctor would not understand what Bobby was to say, so I intervened. 'He cut his hand on a can opener, doctor.' Doctor muttered: 'Can he not speak for himself?' Quick as a flash, Bobby said: 'Whats 'e say?' so I repeated this to him and Bobby said: 'Corse aa can taalk, but a've nivvor hord an accent like ye have, Mr. Doctor, sir.' To add to our amusement, the doctor looked even more perplexed and the nurses were trying hard not to giggle.

126

Doctor then turned to me and said: 'Injection of 10mls of penicillin - then suture it up, nurse.' And off he went. Bobby caught the injection bit and said to me: 'Mind, aa'm not taaking me trousers down for a bit of a lass like you, ne nivvor.' He was adamant, so I gave the injection in his upper arm. For that, I was a 'bonny lass'. As I was inserting the stitches, Doctor came through to check and said: 'Good, good, get him to come back in five days.' I asked Bobby if he could do that, but he said he would be away on stage in Newcastle then. So he said to the doctor: 'Aa can gan to the RVI to have them out.' The doctor asked me what he had said and then condescended to allow Bobby to do just that. I never thought I'd ever be an interpreter between a Tynesider and an Irishman.

Bobby gave me two complimentary tickets to his show for that evening. My fiancé and I went to the Empire and sat in the front row of the circle. I was given a note by the manager to visit Bobby in the dressing room afterwards. In those days, nurses wore outdoor uniform, a navy hat, navy gaberdine coat, black stockings and shoes (keep this in mind as I go on with the story.) Onto the stage came Bobby, in a circle of light, holding up his heavily bandaged thumb. He stood still, looked around the audience, holding out his thumb for all to see and said: 'Eeh, wat a day aa've had. Aa was up at the infirmary 'cos aa cut me thumb, an this young nurse says to me: 'Drop your trousers, Mr Bobby Thompson.' (pause - audience doubled up with laughter) 'Drop me trousers,' aa asked, 'wat for?' 'I'm going to give you an injection,' she said. (pause - even more laughter) 'Eeh, na, you're not, aa'm not dropping me trousers for a slip of a thing like you - aa'm a married man.' 'Eeh, look, there she is up there, the little monkey.' With that, the light shone directly onto me. I thought this was hilarious. The audience clapped and whistled. Then Bobby said: 'An' this doctor, why aa couldn't unnerstand a word he said (pause) 'cos he was Irish, I divvent think the nurses could unnerstand him either.'

After the show, we went to his dressing room and my fiancé had a drink with him. The following morning, I was summoned to Matron's office wondering what I'd done wrong now. I was amazed! She ticked me off thoroughly for making a spectacle of myself at the Sunderland Empire.

'And in nurses' uniform, this is a bad example to your training school, nurse,' she informed me. I was infuriated with Matron, but of course dare not answer back.

'You may go now, nurse, but I shall expect much better of you in the future. If not, you shall be asked to give up your career.' They were her parting words to me.

It was partly due to 'Wor Bobby' that I was able to continue and finish my training, as I made damn sure I was next to perfect in everything as befitted nurses of those days. I was too terrified of Matron's threat to put a foot wrong.

Needless to say, I have repeated this story to lots of people, whenever 'Wor Bobby' was being remembered. We were told later that one of the nursing sisters was in the audience and she informed Matron. My dad thoroughly enjoys this story. He recalls when his father was a steward of a club, in Washington, and little Bobby tried to nip through the back door, unseen, to see the turns on the stage. My grandfather had to turn him out on many occasions, but could never be cross with him as he was such a likeable lad.

When we got married, she walked up the aisle backower because she used to serve ice cream at the Odeon.

PADDY FOX - 'MR FOX'

I was born on June 16, 1914, in Trimdon Street, Sunderland. I went to school at St. Joseph's, in Sunderland. By trade, I was an acetylene burner in the shipyards. I worked all over the area at different places, including the dockyards. For seven years, including the war, I worked for Tyne Dock Engineering at South Shields. I was then employed at Steels for seven years before going to Greenwell's dry-dock, Sunderland.

In those days, you might work all night to get a job finished and the next day you could find yourself laid off. After that, I remember getting a job as a general labourer, sweeping up at Doxfords. The last job I had was at Thompson's, as ship's watch, watching the ropes and putting the lights on in bad weather. It's all closed now, but it was down the dock beside Roker, in Sunderland. Due to arthritis in the spine, I was unemployed for about four or five years before I retired in 1979. I was working when I met Bobby Thompson, but occasionally took the odd day off to be with him on an outing or booking.

The first time I ever met Bobby was around the mid 1950's in a Sunderland club. I think it was the Roker Victoria Club. He came across, we got on talking, got away with each other and 'palled up'. After that, I used to meet him in the Dun Cow when he was on at the Sunderland Empire Theatre. His manager, in those days, was Freddy Rout. They dealt with an agent, called Prenelli, who had premises at the side of Sunderland Empire, as did Freddy, who sold fireplaces in a shop. We saw each other two or three times a week and played dominoes together with Phyllis. I can't tell you why he took to me, he just did. When Lottie was alive, she showed me a cutting from one of Bobby's interviews in which he said: 'Paddy's always by my side'. Phyllis used to come into the pubs where he was playing dominoes and tell someone to go and fetch him because she wanted a drink. I never visited him at home until after Phyllis died, but he often used to come from Whitley Bay, by bus, to my home here in Sunderland. I knew Bobby's sons, Keith and Michael, when they were with him in the family caravan in the Sunderland Empire car park. I think Michael used to go to Cowan Terrace School in Sunderland.

From the time we met, we never had a wrong word and he used to call for me or send a car to pick me up. Usually, it would be one of the other acts that he was on with who would provide the transport. People like Jeff Holland, who later went to Canada. I knew him right through the Tyne Tees series in 1959. He also did the 'One O'clock Show', but I never went to the Tyne Tees studio then. We still saw each other regularly though, and even when he was down, when the series flopped, it didn't affect our friendship. He used to say that I had stuck with him when he was on the bottom and if ever he got back to the top he'd never go back down again - but he started gambling.

I used to accompany him to talent competitions when he couldn't get paid jobs. Sometimes, he couldn't win a one in ages, but he went all over trying to win. He had no transport then, so it was bus and ferry. If the 'Go As You Pleases' were in Sunderland, he spent the night here. If they were north of the Tyne and I was with him, I stayed at his Whitley Bay home when Lottie was his housekeeper. Phyllis, I knew and liked, but had nothing to do with - that was his private life, but she always talked to me whenever we met. They were both heavy drinkers, but when Phyllis died I don't think he touched it after that. He used to drink bitter, and spirits only on rare occasions. Once, he was playing a club at dinner-time when another artist came in and they started to drink brandies. He had another booking at night and I took his clothes up to the club. The concert secretary said Bobby hadn't arrived yet and, if he didn't make it, would I make the apologies to the audience. I told him that I had nothing to do with that side of things. Anyway, they received a call from Bobby, or someone on his behalf, saying that he had to go into hospital.

When Phyllis was very bad, he still had to work, but wherever he was, Middlesbrough, Stockton etc, he used to stop whoever was driving him and phone from a coin box to find out how she was. By that time, she was in a very bad way. I went to the funeral with him and two of his other pals, Pat Healy and Dean Raymond.

He didn't say much about Tyne Tees, or blame anyone strongly, but he wasn't happy about how he was directed, or even the scenery. One small incident sticks in my mind. In one scene, Tyne Tees put the dustbins in the front street and Bobby told them that dustbins in this area were found in the back lane. He had bust-ups with them and told the producer his ideas on how things should have been done.

I was his official dresser, but, as a rule, only performed this duty around the clubs or the Mayfair, Newcastle. I rarely got involved with the pantomime seasons, except in 1979/80 when he played the Newcastle Theatre Royal with David Jason in 'Cinderella'. I used to pack his clothes, army uniform and Little Waster costume, in a certain way and put them out in order on chairs in his dressing-room. After the show, I would pack them away again. His Woodbine packet, containing three cigarettes, was always laid out separately. He timed his act, and its parts, by those three Woodbines. I never saw him smoke anything else but Woodbine cigarettes and occasionally a cigar - if someone gave it to him. Really, me dressing him was a bit of a stunt. It was just to keep me with him - he could dress himself very quickly. Outside, he always called me Mr Fox and I called him Mr Thompson. I got down to London with him three times. One occasion was the 'Same Again' advertising campaign for Vaux. The others were for Lorimers and MFI. I went with him a lot to Billy Botto's Club in Byker, Newcastle, after the Tyne Tees business. Billy Botto gave him regular work and they thought a lot of each other.

He was bitter when nobody wanted him following the TV flop, and used to say that he couldn't win a talent competition to get a cup of tea. On a Sunday morning, after Phyllis died, he used to grab a drink of tea and dash for the train to Hartlepool to do the dinner-time club talent competitions. Many a time, we sat drinking two teas on the train. I used to go through to Newcastle from Sunderland to meet him or, if he was in the area, I would meet up with him at Sunderland station. We both had nothing in those days. He used to say that young Michael had taken bottles back to raise the money for fares. I remember going with him to Pontefract, where he was appearing for the week - we stayed in digs together. When he had the money, he always paid for me wherever we went or stayed.

Although there was no great bitterness over Tyne Tees, what really saddened him was that he felt that when he was down (and often hadn't enough for a smoke, something to eat, or a drink of tea) no one wanted to know him. But when he was on top, then they were throwing money at him. He even used to tell the audiences in night-clubs that I had stuck with him when he was down and out. I always believed that he would climb back because he was so gifted. I don't think that anyone will ever take his place - some try, but he was a 'one-off'.

When Phyllis died, Rosie and I stayed with him at Whitley Bay for five weeks. Brian Shelley took us through. Keith and Michael were still at home, but after he buried her, he just wouldn't let us go home. On the night of Phyllis's funeral, Pat Healy, Dean Raymond, Rosie and I took him out to a pub. I don't know exactly were it was, it was so dark. There was a bit of a concert on. Pat Healy and some of the others were singing, and I think it was Pat who said: 'Get Bobby up,' but Bobby shook his head and said: 'I'm finished, that's knacked me.' But Pat Healy told him to get up and just say a few words. Well, Bobby got up, shook hands with me and Rosie and said this would make him or break him. He was only up at the microphone for a few seconds, said a few words, then came back to our table, shook hands with Rosie and me again and said: 'I think I've made it.' During our stay, he was a bag of nerves and kept the lights burning. I remember going to the toilet in the night and switching off the stairhead light when I came out. Then, I heard his voice call: 'Paddy, Paddy, leave it on.'

He was back on the way up at the time Phyllis died. If he was playing Steels Club, Sunderland, he would stay for Sunday lunch and sleep in the armchair before going out for his evening show. Rosie used to wash and dry his shirt for him, so he was clean to go out. He thought a lot about Rosie. He never forgot us for anything and used to tell people that he had eaten his dinner many a time at our house and was glad of it.

The friendship meant a lot to me, although on the buses people could irritate me by saying: 'Oh, that's Bobby Thompson's mate,' but I never thought about it in that way. We were friends and he was a good friend to me.

Although it never surfaced with me, he had a bad temper and chewed up his supporting act singers two or three times. If he was on the stage, and somebody was singing or talking somewhere, he used to say: 'Could I have a bit of order in there, I never speak when you are on!' He had a good pair of ears on him.

He had a taxi driver who drove him about... it wasn't Ed Simmons. Bobby used to pretend he didn't know the way to places like Wingate Club, saying that he had never been there. After a while on the road, he would ask the driver where he was going. The driver would reply: 'Wingate.' Thompson would then tell him: 'You're miles past it, man, you've cut the slip road out. Do you not get a map?' He'd know where the club was, but he wouldn't tell them. 'They're getting paid and should have a map,' he used to say. He would know if they were deliberately trying to do him. If a singer made fun of an organist, he would pull them and tell the singer not to do that as the organist may have relations in the audience. Bobby was usually polite with everyone who treated him properly and behaved themselves.

We went to one club - Town End Farm, Sunderland - on a Saturday night and there were two wedding parties in the audience. Bobby turned to me and said: 'It's a bit rough here.' We were in the buffet. At first we thought there was just one wedding party in. There was a fellow walking about singing with his shirt hanging out. Alan Durwood was the organist and told Bobby that he shouldn't go on as it was so rowdy. Bobby told Alan that if he didn't want to go on he needn't, but he was being paid and intended to go on stage. Durwood tried to announce Bobby and demand order, but they nearly threw him through a wall. Bobby told him that he was using the wrong tactic, as many of the audience were drunk. Anyway, Bobby gans on and it was so rowdy, mind. 'Somebody getting married here? Hi, Hi, two! What time did you get married?... Half past one... I woulda been in bed by now, man. Enjoy yourselves, never mind me.' The audience went silent - just like that - with his bit of patter. 'Married? enjoy yourselves, have a bit of fun, doesn't matter about little Bobby, man.' You could here a pin drop, just through changing the approach around. He told Durwood: 'You go the wrong way, by demanding that they give order, and you'll get murdered.'

Lottie was a nice woman, a lovely woman she was. I was there when he interviewed her for the job of housekeeper, for him and the two lads. They used to go all over together. Lottie used to come here with him as well. She thought a lot of him. We went on holidays together every year to Blackpool. Rosie and Lottie would play bingo, while Bobby and I went to the betting shop. The betting shop was as far as he went, then we would all go out at night.

He was always recognised in Blackpool and used to enjoy it. We would be sitting in a cafe and people would come and look through the window: 'It is him! Aye, Aye, Bobby.'
'Hello there,' he would say, and go out on to the street to speak to them. 'Where are you from?'
'Durham...' - they used to be pit and colliery places that he knew.

Once, in Whitehaven, Bobby was appearing at a night-club for a week and we were staying in a local hotel. In the evenings, we used to go to the pub before setting off for the night-club. This fella came in, and old pensioner, and Thompson asked how he was keeping. The man told him that his wife was an invalid and they lived in an old people's home nearby. Thompson asked him what he was getting at the bar. The old man told him that he got a bottle of Guinness to take back for his wife and a pie for them to share. Bobby noticed him again on the second night that we went in the pub. After that, he used to buy the old man a pint, then pay for a bottle of Guinness and two pies for him to take back to his missus. He told me: 'You cannot see people beat like that.'

Another time, we were in Pontefract where Thompson was working the week. We were playing dominoes in a pub with an old man and Bobby was winning. The old man said that he would have to go home for his dinner and Bobby asked him if he was coming back out to the pub in the evening. The old man told him that he wouldn't be out as he had no money left, so Bobby dropped him some money to make up for his losses. The next day, the old man came back and Bobby made sure that he filled him with drink. We went to the home where the old man stayed and asked them if we could take him to the night-club. Thompson promised them that he would provide a taxi there and back and look after him, but they wouldn't give permission. He was a good man like that with people.

He was always very careful in case anyone slipped a spirit into his bitter lemon when he got drinks in dressing rooms. 'You've got to be careful no one slips you a Mickey Finn, Paddy,' he used to say. I would have to wash out the glass if he thought that he could smell anything other than the soft drink. He would buy other people spirits and beer, but when he gave up drink he never wanted anything alcoholic. Bobby worried about acquaintances whom he thought drank too much and he used to tell them: 'There's always the next day to drink as much as you want, you spoil yourself like that.' Thompson told me that he reached a point where he knew the drink would do for him, as he was becoming very muddled. That's why he gave it up after Phyllis died.

Nature-wise, Bobby was happy-go-lucky when he was with me, but he was very superstitious. He used to bless himself everytime before a performance, and would twist his rings and touch a special pen he kept for betting on the horses. Before going on stage, he liked me standing near with a bitter lemon or tonic. He didn't like anybody else near him. He used to say: 'Mr Fox, I'm terrified to go near,' but it was all a game, he was having me on. When he was appearing with a big artist, and he knew that they were watching him from the side curtains, he really used to enjoy putting it on: 'Eeh, aa'm just a bag of nerves,' he would say, loud enough for them to hear. The act never took a lot out of him. He told me and others that it was just like anybody talking - 'that's what I get paid for, talking.'

Lottie's death hit him bad. She was so good to him. She put out all his suits and shirts for him - he just had to put them on. She made him wear a bow-tie and got one for me as well. We used to be the same size and I had a regular supply of suits, but he started to go down a lot in weight and later on many of his suits were too small for me.

Mary Douglas was nice and she and Bobby were very pally for some time. I think she came from Annfield Plain, but I'm not sure. I've only been to Annfield Plain once with Bobby, and the club was a hut then.

He could be very untidy in his own home, just take his jacket off and dump it, his shirt and trousers somewhere else. But Lottie didn't care, she just picked them up, brushed them, had them cleaned and set them out again for him. They were always arguing, but it was just like 'God Bless You' to both of them.

When he did pantomime at the Theatre Royal, with David Jason and Leah Bell, he didn't bother much with either of them as he was just the guest artist and they were the players. I used to sign his autograph for him on occasions. At the Royal, he gave me a pile of photo cards and I wrote on them, 'Best Wishes, Bobby Thompson' and gave them out to the crowds at the stage door. They were none the wiser and went away quite happy. I wrote thousands for him and then Cissie said she wanted to write them out. Rosie and I felt that Cissie didn't want us around, but Bobby never knew what was the matter. He asked us why we were stopping away from him. I never said nowt. He asked me if anybody had said anything and I said: 'No.' There was no row. Cissie wanted to start taking his clothes to the dressing-rooms, so I just left it.

He was jealous of his material and used to keep a watch on fellow comedians, in clubs, to make sure that they did not use his stuff. He wouldn't crack the same gag twice when he had close bookings in an area. I used to listen out for gags that he could use. I heard the one about Brendan Foster and the play on the word 'meter'. The bloke on the telly could hardly get a laugh, but Thompson used his voices and made it a winner for him.

He used a mirror to rehearse the different faces he used to pull, and the arrangement of his hair, but he never rehearsed the gags. When he went into a club, he would sit silently and I wouldn't speak to him. People would call out: 'All right, Bobby?' and he would reply: 'Aye, Sunshine, champion, aye'... far away in thought. What he was doing was studying the audience to see what age groups he had, what gags he was going to use, and sorting out their rotation in his mind. He had a good memory and never wrote material down. I would write a joke down for him and he just committed it to memory. Personally, I never had any ambition to be on stage. I'm more like a John Wayne character who just rides away.

Once or twice, he tried to get away from the Little Waster costume and go on in an evening suit. He did this once, when I was with him at Doncaster, and asked me for my opinion after the performance. I had to tell him that it was just not the same. He said: 'I bloody thought so. No more without the jumper.' I told him that I might be wrong and that was only my opinion, but he knew himself. He could come on in the jumper and just stand for five minutes and he got laughs, but you can't do that dressed in an evening suit.

I was with him when he made his records and he enjoyed himself recording them at different places.

In all the years I knew him, I never saw him worry about anything much - including his lads. Our friendship was a close one and I always did whatever he wanted to do. We never argued in all those years and he used to tell his family and everybody about that fact. Thompson was never religious at all, to my knowledge, although he respected his local priest as a man. He was terrified of fights and anything like that, and was always very nervous of those situations.

Communications between us were sometimes a bit awkward. Rosie and I were never on the telephone and he only got one put in after he was taken on by Brian Shelley. He used to phone a neighbour of mine from a call-box and sometimes send me a telegram. At first, receiving a telegram came as a shock, as I thought that something had happened to one of my family, but I got used to getting them from him.

I remember one of his girlfriends, Mabel, but although he liked her, and she was a lovely lass, I don't think that he ever intended to marry her. Although I met him regularly, it was usually during his working hours.

He never worried about the tax, but in latter years he showed me a letter from the tax-man and said: 'Where do they think I'm going to get that?' He was always a gambler and he blew his money. Gambling got the better of him, but even at the casino I would never say anything to him, as that was his personal business. He was going to chuck it three or four times, but never made it. When you see people who have lost their businesses, what chance have you got? It was boring just sitting there for hours at the casino as I never played, just kept him company. Sometimes, Bobby used to take a very old lady, Mrs Parks, who used to have a shop near Princes Gardens many years ago. She used to let Bobby use her telephone before he had one put in his house. Thompson thought a lot of Homer Michaelides at the Casino Royale and they seemed to like him. Some days, he would go there in the afternoon and again in the evening.

After he married Cissie, in 1982, we still saw each other. He would come here, or he would send transport for us to come to Whitley Bay. Our last meeting was just a few weeks before he died. It was a shock when, shortly afterwards, Keith came through to tell us that he was in hospital and that the hospital authorities only allowed family to visit.

Occasionally, he talked about his childhood and told me that it had been a happy one. I remember once when Tyne Tees TV did a programme on him. They took him back to one of his old schools and it brought all the memories back for him for some time afterwards. I met Bobby's brother, Jack, when he was in Sunderland General for a spell. I told Bobby that I would save him the trail through, by visiting Jack and then phoning Bobby with his progress.

He had a good name and was good to people, but could be hard if he had to be. Next to my wife and family, he was the most important person in my life and I miss him a great deal.

PHILIP JONES, PRODUCER OF 'THE BOBBY THOMPSON SHOW' (TYNE TEES TV, 1959)

Yes, of course, with the benefit of another 30 years work in television comedy, I would have advised Bobby differently. Comedy is the toughest area of TV and there are no hard and fast rules. Bobby was certainly not at home in a sketch format and, in retrospect, a better presentation would have been stand-up spots in a variety series. Comics like Arthur Haynes, Benny Hill and Dave King had all had considerable stage experience in sketch comedy, so their transfer to television was easier.

I was not in a position to turn down the brief of a TV series with Bobby, and had no wish to do so. I was quite happy (although nervous!) to accept the challenge. Light Entertainment producers like to have as many viewers as possible watching their programmes and Bobby was a popular name in the North-East.

I really do not recall exactly who offered the Tyne Tees TV series to Bobby. Probably George and Alfred Black, in view of their long association with the area.

I heard Bobby on radio and I am sure I saw him in a club or theatre when the series was suggested.

Actually, my recollection across over 30 years is that the ratings were good - in fact the original planned short run was extended. I cannot say that the series was a happy one to work on - but perhaps that was because I was trying to get a sketch performance (which is acting) from a stand-up comic. No, I don't recall Phyllis interfering at all. My memories are more of Bobby's inability to deliver the dialogue in the right rhythm and with the right stresses. But I don't blame Bobby - we're back to my belief that he was best suited to monologues. As regards drink, yes, I recall a fair amount of Newcastle Brown Ale being consumed, but I do not think it can be blamed for any shortcomings of the series.

I am sure that Bobby respected his supporting performers like Jack Haig, Harold Berens and Len Marten. There was certainly no jealousy or ill-feeling that I can remember.

Of course, it is quite possible that time has mellowed my memories of a series I produced over 30 years ago. Quite possible, because my wife and I spent two extremely happy years in Newcastle and my younger son was born there! Perhaps I have better memories of Bobby and the series than he had of me! The following years, when I was fortunate to work with Frankie Howerd, Tommy Cooper, Benny Hill, Morecambe and Wise and so many other great comics, taught me an ever-increasing respect and admiration for the challenges comedians face.

Bobby was a highly successful and popular performer in his area; he made thousands of people laugh - what better thing can be said?

She said: 'It's them Nigerian kids.'
Aa said: 'Nigeria - where's Nigeria?'
She says: 'Well, it can't be far, they gan home for their dinners.'

DANNY LA RUE

I first met Bobby when I appeared in pantomime with him (1959/60) at the Empire Theatre, Newcastle upon Tyne. The pantomime was 'Cinderella'. Bobby had the main role of Buttons and Alan Haynes and myself were the Ugly Sisters. We had heard of his reputation with North-East audiences and felt a little apprehensive as we travelled up to Newcastle on the train.

When we first met, I suggested that he should have brought a translator. He thought that I was enormously grand and I thought he was a canny bugger.

Bobby liked a drop, as did Phyllis, and he was a terrible gambler. Because of the accent he couldn't transcend into a national comedian, but I have always likened him to the Max Miller mold of nicely naughty. He was also like Chaplin, but most important, Bobby Thompson was of the people.

I remember him affectionately as a scruffy bugger who would have beer bottles on his dressing-room floor and leave his costume where he stepped out of it. I told him that it was unprofessional to treat his clothes like that and he should brush them and place them on hangers after each performance. He was nice to me and used to look at me with that cheeky grin.

He came to see me when I played a Theatre Royal season in Newcastle and I was most touched when he turned up in the queue at a book signing session of mine in the city. He had bought my book and asked me to sign it.

CRAIG DOUGLAS

In the summer of 1961, I was booked for a pantomime season in 'Mother Goose' at Sunderland Empire commencing in the December of that year. Although I was top of the bill, I didn't have a character role but was simply there as a special guest star to attract audiences by singing my record hits. Nat Jackley had second billing playing the Dame and Bobby played the fool's part similar to the Buttons role in 'Cinderella'.

It was a very successful season and Bobby's performance went down a storm; he was tremendous. I knew that Bobby's Tyne Tees TV shows had not been successful in 1959, but here we were seventeen months after the last of those sixteen weekly shows had been transmitted and he couldn't have been more popular with those packed Sunderland audiences. He didn't talk about his TV experience and was never in low spirits during our time together. Bobby's act was so successful that Nat Jackley did not take kindly to his fellow comedian getting the laughs. There was certainly no love lost there. Nat, who had been in showbusiness for some forty years, thought that Bobby was awful and they never socialised during that 1961/62 season. Bobby seemed totally indifferent to Nat's attitude.

My first recollection of him was seeing this small, tramp-like figure arriving late for our first rehearsal. I always do my homework on other acts and researched Bobby after I knew that I had been booked to do the pantomime. Knowing that he was a legend in the North-East, I went up to Sunderland in December 1961 really looking forward to meeting him, learning about him and from him. We took to each other from the beginning. Neither of us had any pretensions about being stars, we were simply at work earning our living. As a general rule in our business, singers love comedy and comedians love singing: Bobby and I were no exceptions.

Unlike many of the great comic talents, he was very likeable and, although I was only twenty, I befriended Bobby from that first meeting.

In turn, Bobby and his family (you got the whole Thompson family when you became friends with Bobby) took to me and became a substitute for my own family during that season.

The Thompsons' way of life interested me, living as they did like gypsies in a little caravan behind the theatre. Phyllis was great, a plump motherly figure who was definitely 'the guv'nor' and ran everything. Clearly, she thought the world of Bobby, but when she was around Bobby tended to do as she told him. The two boys, Michael and Keith, didn't seem to go to school at all during our season although a fortnight or so of that time would have been the Christmas school holidays. They used to treat me like an older brother, follow me around and sit on my knee and talk.

I was booked into a wonderful pub in Silksworth Row, Sunderland for my stay. The owners were great and their place was a haven for theatricals who used to congregate there to see if agents had phoned in any bookings for them. As a newcomer to showbusiness, I was fascinated. During the day, I used to meet up with the Thompsons in their caravan for a chat and a snack. I remember eating a lot of potato crisps with paste spread on them as Bobby used to obtain a supply from a local manufacturer (Hoggets) in return for mentioning their product during his act. At lunch-times, I would accompany the family to a pub next to the theatre. Although I was over eighteen, I still drank orange juice. This was a new world to me and I liked to play dominoes with the company or just sit quietly and listen to them.

At these lunch-time visits, Bobby used to drink very little and not at all if he was doing a matinee performance. He controlled his intake and knew his limits when he was working. The evenings after the shows were different and he nearly always had a hangover when he surfaced between 9 and 10 am the next day. Phyllis liked her drink as well and was always there with him. I never saw him drunk on stage or in the theatre. If he pursued the ladies, I never saw any evidence of it. Bobby was very popular with the locals and an excellent domino player. He was mischievous in a friendly way. When he left a domino game, the others would continue to play - only to find that very often they were one domino short as Bobby had taken it with him.

Phyllis always had a meal ready for him around 5pm and we used to pass any time together before the show by playing darts in the theatre's green room or in the pub.

Although our paths never crossed again, I have such fond memories. Just watching him on stage was an education. His timing, introductions for jokes and handling of the audience were absolutely magic. At first, I found his Geordie dialect hard to understand, but he was so funny visually it really didn't matter. Since that pantomime season, I have gone on to do plays and musicals as well as my singing act. The lessons that I learned from Bobby Thompson have served me well and helped me to do all of those things.

Aa said: 'Aa'm not gannin, it's ower foggy.'
She said: 'Aa can see ower the roof-tops.'
Aa said: 'Aa'm not gannin that way.'

MRS DOREEN DAGLISH

Bobby Thompson came to live in Monkseaton in 1961 when I was working as a barmaid at The Black Horse pub in Front Street. The Thompsons had moved into nearby 20 Princes Gardens, the same house in which my sister and I had been brought up, and The Black Horse became one of his locals.

This would be a couple of years after his Tyne Tees TV appearances when his career was at a low point. Regulars at the Black Horse knew that he was down on his luck, but there was no embarrassment on either side. Bobby was such a funny character that he was quickly liked for himself and not for being a professional entertainer.

When he could afford it, he drank bottles of brown ale or he would 'tick' them (get them on the slate). Bobby would happily accept a drink from other customers, but he never scrounged. In fact, when he had money he would make a point of repaying drinks.

We always had a coal fire going in The Black Horse from opening time. On his way to the bookies or local shops for messages (half a pound of lean mince was a regular item) Bobby would come into the pub through one door, warm his backside, and leave by the other door to continue his journey.

He was really a very private man and I don't think anyone would ever get to know him well. I never met Phyllis, his wife, or Keith, but I knew his oldest lad, Michael, who was a smashing kid and used to come to the side door of the pub looking for his dad. Bobby never talked about Phyllis and I could never imagine him in love with a woman or being romantic. To me, he would be more interested in a woman looking after him like a housekeeper.

Bobby could hold large quantities of beer, but I never saw him the worse for wear. One of his regular drinking mates in Whitley Bay was a lady, Betty, who had a habit of paying for their drinks with bouncing cheques.

Being so naturally funny, I think that those around Bobby allowed him to get away with murder. When he insulted people he had the knack of not being hurtful or offensive. It was all done in a gentle manner.

Even with his trousers secured with a tie around his middle, no socks and old shoes without laces ('because it's the lad's turn to have them'), he had such a cocky walk as if he was the bee's knees. Some of the things that he came out with in normal chat made you wonder whether or not he was having you on. He would come out with statements like: 'Doreen, they've taken down our TV aerial because I hadn't paid for it.' Bobby was deadly serious, hurt and genuinely puzzled that people could behave like that towards him!

After a few years, Bobby's career took off again , but he didn't change his habits, outlook on life or attitude to people. One night, he was appearing at Whitley Bay's Station Hotel and I was in the audience. Unfortunately, during his turn I just had to go to the toilet. Just as I got near to the door, he stopped his routine and said to the audience: 'Do you see that lass there, gannin' in the toilet? Many's the pint Aa've ticked off her.' I could have crawled out. It was a nice compliment and kindly meant, but I didn't see it that way at the time.

On another occasion, in the Seventies, when he was really back on top, he saw three of us on the train going into Newcastle for a girl's night out. He sat beside us for the journey and insisted on taking us for a drink in Newcastle before we started our night.

An' ya knaa when ye get up to stop off.

BRIAN SHELLEY- 'YOUNG 'UN'

I served my time as a plater at Bartram's shipyard, then I went into the Forces for two years. When I came out, I went back to the shipyards before moving on to Steels Cranes. There were an awful lot of people retiring at that time and the company said that they needed somebody to organise some functions. I was in the local showbusiness scene at the time, playing rock-and-roll and piano like Jerry Lee Lewis, so they nominated me and I agreed. Valtino and Val, The Dixielanders and Johnny Duffy were my first acts, then I got The Ryles Brothers on from Doncaster. As a consequence, I met the manager of The Ryles Brothers, Mervyn Oran, who also managed Paul Daniels, David Copperfield and many others. He came to see me and started me off as an agent. I was still working at Steels, but selling acts at night and working week-ends. The business started to move and eventually I took redundancy, which was only £200 at that time, and left Steels to concentrate on the agency.

My first recollection of Bobby Thompson was at the Sunderland Empire, when I was twenty, and I remember that he finished his act by doing a dance, in silhouette, behind a screen with back lighting. It was some years later, in 1966, that our paths actually crossed. Red House Workmen's Club used to do a Monday afternoon show for the night-shift workers, and I was in the club on this particular Monday afternoon when Bobby Thompson was appearing. At that time, there was only myself, the Les Dobinson Agency, Beverley Agency, Joe Mews and Wright. I was sitting with Les Dobinson, and Bobby comes on and he stormed them. I said it was fantastic, and Les asked me if I wanted to meet him. I said: 'Yes, OK.' So, he says: 'Bobby, this is Brian, he is an agent.' And Bobby says: 'Another one like?' (There were five of us then and thirty-six in the peak years of club entertainment.) Apparently, Bobby had just come out of hospital and he had said to Les: 'I'm not working the week-end, can you help us?'
Les said: 'Yes, you can work so and so on Friday night and so and so on Sunday night.'
Bobby said: 'That's fine.'
I said: 'I can give you Saturday night if you want, Bob.'

'Wey, where at like, young 'un?' he asked.

'Pennywell Comrades Club,' I told him. 'Well, how much?' he queried.

'How much do you usually get?' I asked him. 'About fifteen quid,' was the reply.

I said: 'Well, I'll tell you something. You are the best fifteen quids worth I've seen around.'

He said: 'Well, thanks very much.'

I asked him if he would do the booking and he said that he would be there. Of course, I had heard of his reputation. Come Saturday night, I opened the paper... 'Pennywell Comrades tonight - The Bobby Thompson Show'... 'Red House tonight - The Bobby Thompson Show'. Well, I jumped on the telephone to Lance Nesbit who was concert secretary at Red House.

I said: 'Lance, what is going on here, like? I booked him on Monday afternoon for Pennywell Comrades tonight.'

He said: 'Brian, he was booked for Monday afternoon and Saturday night here.'

I said: 'Well, can he double?' Lance said: 'No, sorry.'

Bobby turned up at the Pennywell booking, didn't he. He was only on twelve quid at Red House and he was on fifteen at Pennywell Comrades, and Lance is saying: 'Can he double?' and I'm saying: 'Sorry, Lance.'

After that, I booked him several times. He wasn't on the phone and was living at Whitley Bay. Shortly afterwards, Phyllis died and we went to the funeral. He only waited two or three days before he started working again. I was finding him work and building a reputation as an agent. I was only using good acts. I called my agency The Top Class Agency because I only wanted to use top-class acts, which I did. I've always had good stuff.

Anyway, I said to Bobby (realising that he could give problems, but could also be an asset): 'How about me handling all your work?'

He said: 'Think you could do it?' I said: 'Oh, aye' - quite confident like.

'Well, you're the funniest agent I've ever come across. You find me all my week work, but you get me very little week-end work.' (Of course, mid-week work is the hardest to find.)

I said: 'Well, I'm not really into full steam yet... I've got the office opening, etc.'

He said: 'I'll tell you what - there are two weeks, fill the two weeks.'

He still wasn't on the phone, so he was difficult to get hold of and I was relying on him to ring me. I went to fourteen clubs, and he was barred from ten of them for not turning up. Every club I went into I knew the concert secretary personally, being a singer myself. They knew I was starting off looking for business and I told them: 'Look, I will tell you what I will do with you - if he doesn't turn up, you can kick me out and needn't give me any more business. I'll lay my reputation on the line.' They all accepted that - every one of them. 'How much is he?' they asked. I told them that he was eighteen quid. 'No problem - as long as he is here,' was their reply. They would have paid the world. So, I booked him out and really laid it on the line for him: 'Now look, I have got you into ten clubs that had you barred.' He said: 'You've done weel there, young 'un.' He asked me how much, and when I told him the fee he was knocked out. He wouldn't let me down because he was on top fees all of the time. So, eventually he said: 'OK, you can take over all of the work.' I told him: 'Bob you must get a telephone in, I can't work like this.'

Not long after Phyllis died, I had him on at South Hylton Club and got a phone call at home to tell me that Bobby had collapsed there. I told them that I would come straight to the club, but they said that he had been taken to hospital. Apparently, he had been taking prescribed tablets and drinking. The doctor told me that he wasn't joking when he forecast that Bobby would be dead if he continued to drink alcohol and take his medication. His housekeeper, Lottie, got at him as well, for the sake of his sons. He never drank after that. He really didn't drink alcohol again. In fact, he drank so much bitter lemon that he once collapsed with a bitter lemon in Sacriston Club. Normally, he drank tonic water and people used to think that it was gin and tonic.

When they realised that there was somebody organising him and that he was reliable, his fees just got better and better. All I did to Thompson was organise him and get him good money so that he never let me down. His act was his own - his timing was magic - all I did was direct the business side. I arranged his bookings, guaranteed that he would be there, and got him a singer who had a car so that he didn't have to mess around with taxis. I got him singers who had big flashy cars like Ford Executives and he loved it - Bobby Thompson riding in the back, arriving in style.

In meeting Lottie Tate, and taking her on as his housekeeper, Bobby was a very lucky man. Lottie was a beautiful woman, she really was, and she really looked after him and the two boys. She was as clean as a whistle and so was the house. Bobby was very fond of Lottie and it showed; they had a great friendship. It was sad when she died.

He was the only artist in the North-East who got paid in every venue that he worked. If I let him out to another agent, he would walk in and say: 'Do I get paid?' If they said: 'No, Bobby, we pay the agent'... he would be walking out of the door and they would quickly say: 'It's all right, Bobby, we'll pay you.' He was a clever man.

I helped him get the decorators into his house. They went right through it, and it was beautiful. He was moving up again and he was loving it. I think that he loved the reliability bit as well, because he had been notorious, he really had. After four weeks, he was on £25 a night. The top man in the area at the time was Johnny Duffy, who was on £30, and he was phenomenal as well. He caught level only once with Duffy, and when Duffy found out that Bobby was level he upped his fee again. Anyway, it worked out well.

He had the same costume ever since I knew him. I think that someone did steal an early jersey, but the trousers and cap were his own and were the same ones. Bobby was only doing the one act when I met him - that was the cap and jersey - and he told me that he was thinking of resurrecting another act. I asked him what it was and he told me that it was an Army act and I said that it sounded interesting. He gave me the gist of it and I told him that it sounded pretty good, so he asked me to come along that night and he would show me the routine. Well, he pulled the place apart with it. Next day, I told him that it was fantastic and that he had to keep it in the act. From that point on he did. He told me that he also had another routine, dressed up as a jockey, but I never saw it and he never used it.

At the height of his popularity, his fee in the clubs was between £300 - £500 a night. He did the theatres for £1,000 for one eighteen minute spot: Sunderland Empire, Darlington Civic Theatre and different places. He was really riding the crest of a wave. £500 a night for a club booking! Bobby had it all going for him in 1978, the year his record came out. He had advertising on radio for Starks DIY - 'Gan to Starks', and on television for Vaux. The Lorimer's beer advert, which was filmed in London, earned him £2,000.

The biggest fee of them all came from his appearance as the midnight cabaret in the 1979/80 pantomime, 'Cinderella', at the Theatre Royal, Newcastle. Some years earlier, Bobby had said to me: 'Listen, if you can get the chance of a pantomime I don't mind them, but Buttons is too heavy for me at my age.' He was too old to go on and off stage and do all the changes, that is why he told me never to put him in for that part. I agreed and forgot about it until 1979 when I got a phone call from Michael Grayson at the Theatre Royal.

'I've got this idea,' he said, 'I would like to put Bobby on the pantomime with David Jason and Leah Bell.'

I asked him which pantomime and he told me that it was 'Cinderella' and Bobby would be playing Buttons. I told him that it was a hard role and would cost him a lot of money - trying to put him off. He asked me what we were talking about in money terms. I told him that he was looking at about £5,000 a week.

He said: 'Mmmm, you can leave it with me and I'll come back to you.' He came back saying: 'Yes, that's OK, we can manage that.' I told him that I would have to speak to Bobby about this and rang him. I told him that he wasn't going to believe me, but that I had got him five grand a week at the Theatre Royal. He said: 'You what!' I told him that I had got him five grand a week, but it was for playing Buttons.

He said: 'I can't, Brian, I'd love to, the money's fantastic.' I asked him if he would leave it with me and would he be satisfied if I could get him half of that for one slot. He said: 'That'll be fabulous, young 'un,' and left me to it.

I rang the Theatre Royal and said: 'Look, you are only using Bobby to pull them in aren't you?' He said: 'Oh, yes, yes.' I said: 'Why don't you just use him for one spot and we will halve the fee?' He thought that was fantastic and accepted it - one eighteen minute spot for two and a half grand a week. Well, I mean!

It was my suggestion, in 1978, that he release a long playing record. He said that if he did that, then everyone would know his act. I laughed and told him that everybody knew his act anyway. I told him that I could do his act and I still can. He said that he was a bit wary about the record, but I told him that he would make a fortune. So, I rang Dave Wood, who was a friend of mine, and told him the idea. Dave said that he had been tossing the same thought around himself, so we sat down, discussed it and made the record, "The Little Waster" - you know what happened. In the North-East, "Grease" was out at the time. Bobby was outselling John Travolta and Olivia Newton-John, two albums to one. He even made the national charts at one point, which was unusual.

In the clubs and theatres, everybody would always ask whether he would turn up - you always got this question. I would say to them that he had never let me down yet. I think that he only let me down three times in nineteen years. As I have already mentioned, he collapsed on stage at South Hylton and obviously the next night he couldn't work. Even then, they wouldn't believe me because the club had a full house and didn't want excuses. On another occasion, he arrived at a venue but was unable to climb several flights of stairs to get into the club. The remaining occasion, however, was certainly his fault, but he learned his lesson from the experience. I was doing well with Bobby and had got him back into most places where, before our association, he had previously been barred for not turning up. Anyway, I was doing the bookings for Hardwick Hartley Social Club, Stockton, and it was a difficult club to book. Their concert secretary, Billy Sharp, could be difficult to deal with, but I got on with him. They were short of an act for Monday and I had Bobby available. Unfortunately, the club had barred him some years before and I had tried for years to get him back in, but they weren't having any of it, even when he was successful. Sharpey used to phone me and say: 'What rubbish have we got this week-end then, young 'un?' I used to say: 'Weel, you've got so and so Saturday, Sunday morning someone else.' 'What about Monday?' Sharpey asked. I told him that I was still looking for a good show, but that I had Bobby available. He told me that 'the little bastard' wouldn't turn up. I told him: 'Billy, he has never let me down yet.' I told him that if Bobby didn't turn up he could kick me out. 'Go on,' he said, 'stick him in.'

Bobby came in on the Monday morning to pay me his previous month's commission. He used to shake my hand and thank me for the work, collect his list of venues, and away he would go as happy as Larry. I didn't hear anything till Wednesday when Sharpey rang me.

'Is that you, Shell? The little bastard's done it again.' I said: 'You're joking.' He said: 'I'm not joking, bonny lad. They were standing ten deep at the bar, sitting on the windowsills. I couldn't believe the people in here, and he let me down.' I got Lottie Tate on the other line and told Sharpey to listen to the conversation.

'Lottie, is Bobby there?' She said that he wasn't... poor soul, she was covering up for him. 'Just tell him that he doesn't do that to me. He has got his work until Saturday and after that he finds his own.'

She said: 'OK, Brian, I'll tell him.'

I asked Sharpey if he had heard and he said: 'Shell, I appreciate that. I know what you said, but I'm not blowing you out.'

I told him: 'Thanks a lot,' and he said: 'Well, your entertainment has been steady and I'm happy' - so away he goes.

I was raving... you can imagine. I didn't hear anything from Bobby until Saturday morning. The phone rang and I was in a different mood, relaxed.

'Brian, hold on, and before you speak, I was wrong, I was way out of line. I should never have done that. I promise you that I'll never do it again. What do I have to do to put it right?'

I said: 'You ring Sharpey... I don't care if you have to work for nothing, or if you have to work for half-fee. I don't care what you do it for, but you ring Sharpey.' Actually, I was still looking for a show for Monday night as it was a hard club to book.

'Aye, OK.'

He rang me back: 'That's OK, it's fixed up.'

Then Sharpey comes on to me: 'Is that you Shell... will he turn up?'

I told him that I didn't want to know and that I had told Bobby to sort it out with him.

Sharpey said: 'OK.'

So, Bobby turned up on the Monday night. Again, they were standing ten-deep at the bar and sitting on the windowsills. The little man comes on and says: 'Hello there. Half of you have come to see me and the other half of you have come to see if I turned up.' The place went up!

I used to own a racehorse called Paintbox, but Bobby had nothing to do with that at all. Mervyn Oran and I shared the horse between us, but Bobby used to go around saying that it was part his. It ran about twenty-two times in the two years. It came second five times, third five times and fourth five times, but we never got a winner out of it - which is why Bobby used to say, in some quarters, that it only had three legs.

The club scene had been dying for some time and I could see the writing on the wall. By 1984, I had decided to diversify my business interests by taking on the running of three pubs while still operating my agency, but on a smaller scale. It was no longer good business practice to handle large volumes of bookings, because it forced you to lay out too much money. The acts would come down from Scotland or up from the Midlands. If you got a band and they were on £1,000 a week, then they would want their £1,000 at the end of the week, but an agent didn't see the money from the clubs for six or seven weeks. That was only for one band, so you can imagine that multiplied. The overdraft that you needed, to cover the money you had out, was crazy. There were agents with £40,000 overdrafts.

In 1985, looking after the pubs and Bobby's career was heavy going, but I was on top of the work and made sure that Bobby wasn't neglected. I

154

used to set out in writing all of his venues for the month ahead and, in fact, he had work booked in for the rest of that year. Theoretically, that should have been enough for him, but he liked to talk everyday. He would ring me up in the morning ('Hello, Brian, ...') and talk about the night before or whatever. I was never renowned for my patience with anybody, but with Bobby I just had this thing - we got on well and it didn't matter how much he upset me, I really didn't get angry. We had this relationship where we were good for each other. He opened a lot of doors for me due to the fact that I handled him and he was a star.

Bobby phoning me everyday I didn't mind. In fact, I always appreciated that he liked to chat to me, but it was the frequency of the calls. If he was on the phone once a day, he was on twelve or thirteen times. Anyway, the inevitable happened and he phoned me when I was having a bad day. I told him: 'Bobby, you've got all of your venues, you know where you are working.' He said something to me which irritated me and I said: 'Look, if you feel like that, then get the work yourself, if that is what you want.' 'Right,' he replied, and I realised that it had all been lined up and someone had lined it up for him. I was taken aback as he had all his work scheduled way ahead. If he hadn't, then I could have understood.

The next thing I knew, he asked me for all of his venues and I gave them to him. I didn't get paid any commission from that day on and he must have owed me a grand for what was lined up for him. Shortly afterwards, I was talking on the phone to Ronnie Vaughan of the Lewis Vaughan Agency. I told him: 'Congratulations,' and asked whether he knew what he had taken on. He said: 'Well, you know.....' I said: 'Wrong, bonny lad - it's a relief to me because he needs so much attention.' I told him that he would rue the day. After about four weeks, I was talking to Ronnie again and he said: 'You were right, there!'

I didn't want to let Bobby go to the Lewis Vaughan Agency. Over the years, all the other agents had tried to steal him away, but he wasn't daft. You never leave something that is good. I'm not being big-headed, but no other agent could have handled him as I did. Bobby was a very difficult man to manage, and the older he got, the more difficult he became. It was nothing for him to ring up, with the bookings in front of him, and say: 'I'm not on tonight, Brian.' I used to tell him: 'Bobby, it's confirmed.' Then, it would be a different tack: 'I'm not going to work with him ...(etc).' So, that is how he left me. Sadly, in the end, I think that our split was inevitable. It was that kind of situation, you couldn't run your business and give him all the attention that he wanted. He was so lonely, he just wanted to talk about everything and nothing all day.

Let me tell you about his pièce de résistance during our time together. I got a phone call from Bobby telling me that there was this guy who wanted him to work the Palladium. He gave his name... Charlie Lee... and asked me to give him a ring. I said: 'OK,' and phoned the man. I said: 'You want Bobby?' and he explained that he was putting on a Geordie show and he wanted Bobby to top the bill. This incident was after his Wimbledon Theatre and 'Wogan' appearances and near the end of his time with me. Charlie told me that he would give us £1,000 for one spot. Well, his money had come to a lower level at that time, so I rang Bobby, asked him if he wanted to do it, and told him that it was £1,000 for one spot. I knew how to handle him and, as I didn't want any problems, would never book in anything without checking with him first. He said: 'Aye, OK,' he would do it. When he was in London to do 'Wogan' and the Wimbledon Theatre Sunday concert (which probably gave rise to the Palladium offer) he had called at the Palladium and was shown around by the theatre manager. At that time, Russ Abbot had his show on and he had a crack with Bobby, having known him from his own North-East club days.

The next week, after we received the Palladium offer, Bobby rang me. Remember, this is the Palladium we are talking about - the ultimate in British entertainment. He said to me: 'Have you seen who the support is, bonny lad?' I said: 'Personally, I don't give a toss, you're there for 18 - 20 minutes.' 'It's Leah Bell,' he said. He didn't like Leah Bell. I don't know why, but it went back a long time. Although she is a lovely kid, they just didn't hit it off.*

* Author's note: Leah Bell stated that she was unaware of any discord.

156

'I'm not working with her,' he stated.

I told him that he had to be joking. He said that he wasn't and that I could take the booking out.

I said: 'You're talking about the Palladium, Bobby. People work the Palladium for nothing - just to say that they've worked there.'

He told me that he wouldn't work with Leah Bell and to take it out. I told him that I would talk to him at the back end of the week, but he was adamant that he wasn't going to work with her.

I said: 'You know what you'll do? I'll cancel this and you'll be back in two days time telling me to put it back in.'

'Take it out,' he said.

I told him: 'OK, Bobby.' I then sent him a letter stating, as he had requested, that I was cancelling the booking. I rang Charlie and told him that he wasn't going to believe this, but that Bobby didn't want to work with Leah. Charlie said: 'Look, just take it out, I cannot stand the hassle' - because Bobby had been on the phone to Charlie every day about it as well.

I rang Bobby and told him that I had already sent him a letter confirming that I had cancelled the booking and now I had sent a similar one to Charlie, so the show had been formally cancelled. The rest of the acts were all Beverley artists, but I didn't mind.

Bobby came back to me two days later telling me that Charlie wasn't going ahead with the show. I told him not to come to me and that I had given him lots of warnings and even set it out in writing to him. He got annoyed. Fancy, turning down the Palladium because he didn't like the supporting acts!

As his manager and agent, I always stuck to 10 per cent commission for a few reasons. First, 10 per cent of five grand is better than 15 per cent of a few hundred. On top of that, he was excellent for business. If anyone rang for Bobby, I could sell them someone else as well.

He never liked to work with a strong support. If I was putting on acts like Dave Green (£100) and Bobby (£200) that the club asked for, because they felt it was a stronger show, he would say: 'Listen, you can put my singer on with me, and you can give me all the money and I'll pay him.' That is the way he looked at it. He used to tell me: 'Look, it's me that is filling the clubs.' That was his argument and he was quite right, but to the clubs the singers weren't strong acts. However, Bobby felt that putting a strong singer on before him was a threat to his act. That was ridiculous because really it made the whole show better. It didn't matter who was on the bill, they went to see Bobby - not the support.

There was no great social relationship between us. I would meet up with him or see him around the clubs twice a month or he would ask me over to his home for a chat. He knew my wife and that was about it.

He was a businessman - at one time he had £160,000 and some property. I put a safe into the Monkseaton house for him. One time, I went across to pick up my commission and he had ten-pound notes and twenty-pound notes hanging out of the teapot and jars. I said: 'Bobby, you cannot do this, you need a safe.' He asked me to get him one. I lined it up and got the safe put in for him. I went back to his home about three months later and he still had these twenty-pound notes in the teapot and glasses. 'Bobby, man, you've got a safe now,' I said. And he said: 'Brian, man, it's full.' He had that much money, it was coming out of his ears.

Bobby once told me that he had had a lot of managers in his time, but that I was the best and the most consistent. I had done a good job for him and he was praising me. If I walked into a club when he was on stage, he would say: 'Ladies and gentlemen, that is my manager, could I have a big hand, he does a great job.' He would always do that kind of thing for you.

We never had a contract in all those years. They aren't worth a light, anyway. The point is this, if I can't hold onto an act through the business I bring in, and the personal relationship, then it is going to disappear anyway.

He was a lonely man - that is why he was on the telephone so much. He could sit in his house with whoever, but in my time the only one who filled his life was Lottie. He really thought the world of Lottie and was cut up when she died. He would sit and talk with her and carry on, and there was genuine happiness there - that is what I could see when I went across to his home.

Regarding charities, my argument is that if a man is a star then everybody wants him for charity - and every charity is deserving, but it was my job as a manager to make sure that he had an income. I used to plan so many charities a month and say to them: 'Bobby will do the charity and he wants half-fee.' If they listened to what I had to say then they would make money, and they did. He used to fill places and they used to come back again and say: 'We did great, that was excellent.' I have a boy who is deaf and dumb and I used to run charities for the deaf, but Bobby always got half-fee. I think that is being a good manager - looking after your act. He did some work for nothing, like the Empire Theatre, Sunderland, for the old people, and more - but there is a limit to what I would allow to happen.

One charity event really sticks in my mind. When Muhammad Ali came over in July, 1977, Bobby phoned me to say that one of the organisers had asked him to do the cabaret at the Thursday night banquet. He said he had a couple of tickets and did I want one. I told him that I would love one and could he get another one for my wife. He told me to leave it with him and then rang me back to say that he had another ticket, but I would have to pay for that one. I was pleased and told him that paying for the ticket wasn't a problem. We went to the banquet. There was a singer, Bobby, a compere and somebody else. So, I'm standing talking to a group of people who asked me how Bobby was doing. Well, I shouldn't have done, but I really laid it on. He was due to have a long playing record out, he put more people in one of the theatres that he played for a week when people like Tom Jones couldn't fill it... I really went to town. Within minutes, I was told that Bobby was not to go on, and he didn't appear!

Some clubs used to approach him and he would agree to a date, forgetting that he was already booked in elsewhere. Then he'd say: 'Oh,

Brian, I've forgotten to tell you...' I'd have to sort it out. I got quite skilled at it at the finish. The High Pit Social Club dispute came about because of such an arrangement. He made his own deal with them, to appear for something like £300, and pulled out when he found out that other household names were getting considerably more and the club wouldn't increase his fee. He genuinely felt that the other acts were on the way down and he was at his peak and could fill the seats better than they could.

We never spoke after the split, which was ridiculous. I don't think that our paths crossed again. The next time I saw him, they were putting him down a hole. I lived in Spain for nearly two years and when I came back he was in hospital. The next thing I knew, he was dead. I rang Cissie and Keith to ask if they had any objections if I came to the funeral and both said I was welcome.

I never thought that I could push him nationally. You could only push him as far down as you could find North-East exiles. He could go down to Nottingham, or any pit places where the lads had moved to find jobs. Even the London job, at Wimbledon, was for exiles.

He was a very good mimic and could have adopted a middle accent, but he was not a funny man. He was a man who told funny stories and did them well. Nobody could do them better, but if you asked him to crack a gag he couldn't. He wasn't a comedian, he was a story teller. If you want to prove the point, dig out the tape for 'Wogan' or see an interview with Tyne Tees. He used to be Mr Prim. He would put it on, and if they wanted him to be funny he used to do a line from his act. Bobby always only did a line from his act. He couldn't stand up at a bar with Johnny Hammond - who is better at the bar than he is on the stage. Bob didn't crack jokes at the bar, he would pull a one-liner from his act.

Professionally, as funny men go, his biggest asset was his timing and delivery. Everybody in the business commented that his timing and delivery were exceptional. He wrote all his own material and, putting it all together, he was brilliant, but it was all stories. Bobby didn't have to vary the act because that is what people wanted to hear. They would ask him for the one about this or that, just like Tom Jones being asked to sing his hits.

It was a privilege to handle the North-East Legend, it really was a privilege.

It's about four years since we were speakin' properly and she says to me: 'Darlin' ('cos the window's open), are we going to Blackpool for our holidays?'

So, I shut the window. Aa says: 'Keep ya clagger shut. How can we go to Blackpool on the money you're making.' Then, I opened the window. Aa says: 'Where are we flying from?'

Well, she wanted to fly from Shotton. Aa says: 'We'll fly from Horden, then we can stop at Peterlee and refuel.'

FATHER RICHARD CASS

Long before I ever met him, I knew Bobby from his recordings on the radio. Also, I worked with a priest, in Consett, who had spent some time in Penshaw, and he told me that Bobby and his family originated from the area. He had a brother there, called Jimmy, who was a great help to us, being very much involved in the life of the community and the church. That is really how I became very interested in Bobby.

When I came to Whitley Bay in 1973, I knew that he was living in the area and visited him on my ordinary rounds. I found Bobby to be a man without any pretence. He was always himself and did not want to be anything else. People who were able to accept him as he was, and who he was, and where he was, became a friend of Bobby's. My belief is that he found that acceptance in me and felt that he could communicate with me. Certainly, we could really relate very well to each other. He had a great flair for sport, particularly for horses, and I came from a part of Ireland where we were brought up with horses. We had quite a lot in common and we'd sit and talk about all those things. Bobby was a man who liked excitement in his life, and whatever brought that excitement to his life he was very much a part of it.

Regarding any deep conversation with Bobby, we spoke about everything. He was very clear in the way he thought about all the hardships he could see in the world, and was deeply moved by any kind of tragedy that came into the lives of people. Not only the tragedies abroad, but the tragedies of life. I found that Bobby was always willing to help in such cases. He was very considerate to people in the sense that everyone meant an awful lot to him. I didn't pester Bobby to do charities for me, but Bobby would always say that whenever I needed such work he would be pleased if we contacted him. When we did, there was no doubt about it that Bobby would never take a penny. I found him extremely generous.

If you ask whether Bobby was a religious man, I would say there is a big difference between a religious man and a person that has Christ in his life - a Christ-like person. I would say that Bobby was a Christ-like man in many ways because he had the love of Christ in his heart and could be moved to compassion. He could relate to people and be himself with people. He would never put on a show, it was the real Bobby Thompson whenever they met him. We never parted without speaking about God, about our relationship with God and what God meant to both of us in our lives. Bobby would say: 'I haven't been to St. Edward's as often as I should have been,' but there is no doubt that Bobby had been many times to St. Edward's in my time here. However, I don't judge a man on the number of times he has been to church, but I judge him on the generosity of heart and the way he reaches out to other people with his compassion. I always found that in Bobby and spoke about that quality at his funeral. The final judgement is going to be based upon how we related to other people. The Bible is quite clear, the good we do to others, we do to Christ. That is why I say that Bobby will be rewarded with the fullness of life with God, because he did all those things to people who were in need.

As regards his relationships outside, we never discussed anything regarding his love life. But you ask how his life as a showbusiness personality could be reconciled to the ways of the church? I felt that Bobby was a great ambassador for what showbusiness should be. There is one particular incident I know of, when Bobby was booked to do a show in a Sunderland club. When he got there, he was told there was to be a stripper on the show with him. Bobby said to her: 'Now, either ye gan or I gan, because I'm not gannin' on wi' you.' Bobby packed his bag and came away. He had his own standards of morality in that way and always felt that his humour and art were natural, and that he didn't have to resort to anything that was immoral or objectionable to entertain people. I always admired him very much for that. Wherever Bobby Thompson was performing, I would feel very safe in bringing my grandmother, my mother, anybody, to listen to his show.

Probably he had a kind of carefree attitude to life and this would give people the feeling that he couldn't care less, but Bobby wasn't like that. He thought of death and life hereafter, but didn't approach it in a morbid way. Bobby lived his life to the full, as he thought it, without doing any injustice to his fellow men and trying to help them as best he could. That is the way he was preparing for the next world. During his last illness, when he was admitted to hospital, I was the first man he sent for and he wanted to be supported by all the help the Church could give him. He wanted to put his life before God and to receive the strength of the sacramental life of the Church, and he was blessed with that.

I was talking to one of his sons recently, and he told me how much Bobby thought of me as a person. Being told this by a member of his family gave me much pleasure. He admired everything that I stood for and did. He wouldn't belittle that in any way. Whenever I met Bobby, wherever I was, Bobby would come over to me and was always delighted to see me, to introduce me to his friends, and be very proud of the fact that we were friends.

However, with regard to his approach to religion and whether he could have been influenced more by the singer (me) than the song, I would say that wasn't Bobby's approach. Above everything else, he was a very sincere man, and was born a Catholic from a Catholic family.

Bobby never turned his back on what he was. He didn't belittle anyone in his life. He mixed with the highest, and he mixed with people who were unfortunate and those on the margins of society. He had great compassion and a great regard for the dignity of the human person.

Aa wasn't ganna turn out. Aa didn't turn out till quarter to six.

And ye knaa, the women sit there. They cannit smell your dinner burning, but they can smell money.

TONY SANDS

My interest in showbusiness goes back over thirty years. I used to work as a croupier in a night-club and we used to get all of the acts coming in. Suddenly, I knew that I wanted to be an entertainer. For years I had thought that I could do it, so I set about achieving my ambitions, like most acts, by doing 'Go As You Please' competitions in workingmen's clubs. It was in the clubs that I first came across this comedian, Bobby Thompson. In those days, I was a total amateur - I didn't have a clue - and I used to watch this man on stage who was top of the bill. My admiration was instant.

Some years later, when I'd got my singing act together (the hypnotism act came later) and turned professional, I found myself working with Bobby Thompson. To me, this was like working with a star. But Bobby could never really get out of workingmen's clubs because of the Geordie accent. I'm not sure that he ever wanted to travel in any case. He was a great character, and a little story comes to mind when I was supporting Bobby on a club bill around 1964/5. At the end of our show, he came over to me and said: 'Hi, you're a canny singer, lad. What do you think about working with me all the time?' I thought to myself, this will be great - working with Bobby Thompson, I'll have loads of work. He was working every night, whereas I was only working two or three nights. I told him I was interested and Bobby said: 'Well, ye knaa, I think we'd do well, me and ye together. You've got a good voice and good presentation, a nice opening act for me.' Then he said: 'Have you got a car?' I said: 'Yes, naturally, I've got a car.' In those days I was carrying PA equipment and microphones around. He said: 'Oh, weel, that's great, you can pick me up and take me to and from the venues ye knaa.' I said: 'Oh, yes,' and more or less agreed. A couple of days later I mentioned the conversation to another singer who said: 'Oh, no, not you as well!' I said: 'What do you mean, not me as well?' He said: 'He does that to everybody.' I said: 'You're joking.' 'Look,' he said, 'Bobby hasn't got a car and he hasn't got a driver. If he has to use a taxi it costs him money, whereas if he has another act working with him who has a car, travelling to and from his bookings doesn't cost him anything!' I said:

'The bastard!' I thought his offer over carefully, but realised that, inspite of the extra wages, I couldn't be bothered with the hassle of chauffeuring him around. Not that I didn't enjoy working with him, he was fantastic. On a personal basis, I never got to know him and never visited his home. What I knew of Bobby came solely through working with him.

Bobby Thompson as an act was essentially visual. Very few people can walk on stage and just stand there causing the audience to fall about laughing. Why do they react in that way? In my opinion, it was because of his funny clothes, whether he was dressed like a tramp or in a soldier's uniform, and his facial expression with his hair lying over his one funny eye. I worked many times with Tommy Cooper and he had the same gift. If that visual talent had been taken abroad, worked on and properly publicised, he could have topped the bill anywhere. I put his trouble with the Tyne Tees shows in 1959 down to those in charge trying to change his act for a new medium. In my opinion, they simply didn't understand Bobby Thompson. Everybody knew what he was going to say and the punch lines didn't matter. It was the visual effect and how he told his stories. I can't understand why his statue doesn't stand in Northumberland Street, Newcastle, or why he hasn't had a North-East theatre named after him. It's the old saying: 'You can't be a prophet in your own land.'

Bobby liked to gamble and I've known the Michaelides family, who ran the Casino Royale in Newcastle, for many years. I used to entertain at some of their staff dances and on one of these occasions, when Bobby was a guest, I hypnotised a croupier to do Bobby Thompson's act. The guy went through Bobby's routines perfectly and Bobby was sitting there, in his dinner suit, laughing his head off.

In clubland, if you arrive in a good suit they think that your act must be good. Bobby would come in wearing an immaculate dinner suit and try to put on this awful posh accent - which doesn't work if you're a Geordie. Then he would go into the dressing room and put on his scruffy stage gear. He was the exact opposite of the other acts. When he came off the stage and put his dinner suit back on, the transformation was absolutely incredible - it wasn't the same man.

I learned a lot from Bobby, but the most important thing he taught me was how to bring yourself down to the audience, so that they feel you are one of them and that they know you. You can't go into a workingmen's club and try to be a big international star, it doesn't work. You can dress and present the act well, but you've got to look down into the audience and say: 'Are you all right there, Missus?' That is what he had. He associated and identified with people.

She's gone with the wind, man.

Mind, aa'll tell you something, these knockers that comes to your door on a Friday night want spifflicating. Pouring wi' rain ya knaa, they nivvor tak a holiday.
They come to your door wi' the book open! Open! The brazen lookin' b...
And they'll stand there. They're there, lad.... and they knaa ya're not in.
Let them knock - the paint lasts langer than the skin.

If debt was a disease, she would be in the best of health.

DAVE WOOD

I never actually saw Bobby Thompson perform before being involved with him. Obviously, I had heard about him, but I didn't know a lot about him until I was asked by Brian Shelley, who I had known for a long time, about the chances of putting together an album of his material. I went and had a discussion with them and we worked out how we could record and issue it. Things then moved very quickly. We recorded "The Little Waster" in 1978 at Ryhope Poplars Club, Sunderland, and then at the Mayfair Ballroom, Newcastle. In fact, we didn't record much more - I think we did one other date and issued the album in the October of that year. Within a month, we couldn't cope with the demand, it was quite fantastic. Towards Christmas of that year, Bobby was selling faster than the number one album, "Grease", in the North-East area. It really took off and boosted Bobby beyond all recognition.

It was quite interesting, as I took the album to a local record shop as a kind of: 'Oh, I'll go in and see what they think.' The girl in the shop said: 'I don't think that will do anything.' I was a little disappointed that she didn't have any more to say about it than that. A few days later, she is knocking on the door asking if she can buy twenty-five! It just went mad from there. The record shops would be on the phone every morning ordering up and the people handling the distribution had a right job on their hands.

He wasn't difficult to record because he was very professional. In fact, that is one of the things that impressed me. His delivery and script, that he had obviously developed over the years, were spot-on and the timing was brilliant. He could probably do his act in his sleep, he was that good. Everybody thought the world of him and loved him because he was just talking about everyday life in the past. Some of it was current as well, and he would always drop the odd little name in to cause an effect. He really had a tremendous act, and on the album I don't think there was anything cut out, except perhaps the odd cough and splutter from years of smoking Woodbines. The first album was a true picture of his act.

He appealed to both older and younger audiences. Even younger ones understood about debt. He always had them laughing. He kind of thumbed his nose at the system as far as I could see, although I never really knew him well. What came over was that he was his own person, and I gather from the past that he had been in and out of all sorts of hassles. His act was very near to what he had experienced, I would say.

With hindsight, the decision to record him was a good judgment. However, at the time, we really didn't know how it would go as it was something quite unique. It seemed as if it was a piece of history and worth giving a try.

In terms of sales, the album quickly did 20,000, but Brian Shelley would be better placed to give the financial side of it. I know that when we did the second LP, "The Bobby Thompson Laugh In", we improved the deal for Bobby so that he got more out of it. That move would come from Bobby and I don't blame him. He was a stickler for his earnings. It was his career, his job, and he knew his worth. We did just two albums and a single, "When I was a Lad", which was an Eric Boswell song. There was a précis of humour thrown together on the B side, a sort of collage, as a promotion for the album. The single didn't do much. "The Little Waster" is the Bobby Thompson album which didn't take much to put together. "The Laugh In" album did take a lot of compiling as we had to look for new material and that was a problem. We all realised that new material wouldn't go down too well because it wasn't what people were waiting to hear. I think from the number of times I saw him, I could probably recite his act, but I would still enjoy listening to it now as I did then, it was absolutely unique.

The second album only sold about 10,000 copies. A lot of people didn't know that it existed. We spoke to Richard Kelly to get some new lines and gags to use on the second and managed to get a bit of stuff together. Then, we went out for a couple of consecutive nights to record Bobby using the new material, which he threw into his regular routines, so that we had it covered. It took a long time and I had a lot of difficulty assembling it.

Promotionally, we had no trouble. People used to bring their albums for him to sign in the clubs and coverage in the newspapers and shops was immense. I remember once going to Woolworth, in Sunderland, and I reckon that in about an hour they must have sold a hundred albums and he signed them all. Sometimes, we used to do two or three of those appearances a day. The shop managers all treated him with great respect and looked after him. They always had a cup of tea ready and a prominent display with posters and sleeves. He was made comfortable and they didn't ask him to do too much. Bobby was great at these appearances, but I think, when we started to do a few, he could have done with not diving around like a rock star. He always enjoyed people's interest and treated his public well.

We did have little set to's with him over bits and pieces. He might have been to a shop and his record was out of stock and, inevitably, it was very difficult for us to cope with the demand for his first LP. Somebody would tell him that they couldn't get his record at such-and-such a shop and he would come to me and say that half the street had been trying unsuccessfully to buy his record. It was difficult, we had something like six record plants trying to press it and it was just before Christmas so we were trying to keep up with the demand. One pressing plant took an Elvis Presley record off the presses to put a Bobby Thompson record on. They would have got their fingers rapped for that if it had ever come out. He really was 'listenable' for any age group and didn't like people with vulgar material. He would never stand for that, which I thought was great - a comic who had absolutely clean material in that day and age.

The videos of his acts were produced by Tyne Tees TV. The video is just his stage show on tape. That went down extremely well. Tyne Tees sold quite a few copies of that.

I think, as Bobby rightly said, his accent kept him in the North as Southerners probably couldn't understand a lot of it. That said, I think that with programmes like 'Auf Weidersehen Pet' and others making the North-East accent as well known as those of Manchester and Liverpool, perhaps someone like Bobby would stand more of a chance now than he did then. The Geordie accent is now widely accepted.

We did have a contract to produce three albums with Bobby, but I told Brian that I didn't think that there was a third album there. We have some unreleased songs in the studio. I remember "HMS Hood" and some Eric Boswell songs. He was never really a singer. I suppose the music hall tradition is for a comic to end up doing a song, but if you had to give him percentages for his act you would give him 200 per cent for his comedy and 20 per cent for his singing.

I knew Lottie quite well, she really looked after him and was a nice lady. Paddy was his dresser, carrying his case in and out; putting his stuff out for him, his jumper and his Woodbine packets. He didn't have a lot to do. Bobby just used to go and get changed quickly - he always had his long johns on. It was wonderful. The compere would say: 'Ladies and Gentlemen, a big round of applause, a keen welcome for Bobby Thompson.' The spotlight would go over to where he was and he would just shuffle on, fags in hand, and grin. Everyone would just burst themselves. He would then move to the mike and say: 'Are you all right?' From the word go it was always funny and I can never remember seeing him when the audience wasn't on the floor.

"The Little Waster" album did most of its business in the first year or so. As the second one didn't have the same impact, I didn't see a lot of him after that. He would ring up and ask how things were going and I'd have a chat with him - not a lot else, really. Knowing that we weren't going to do a third album, there was no point in pursuing anything, rather get on with something else.

Outside, he'd always buy me a drink or if I went down to his house he was very hospitable. He always liked to make people feel comfortable. We didn't really socialise and he wouldn't want to socialise with me and vice-versa. It was always pleasant doing business with him.

I always thought that it was a shame that his success came when it did. After all, if you get a bit of fame and fortune at that age you cannot go windsurfing or para-gliding, which you might do if you were a bit younger. I felt that he was irritated that it hadn't all come a bit earlier to him, for I'm sure he would have made better use of it.

171

DAVID JASON

During the 1979/80 pantomime season, I appeared as Buttons in 'Cinderella' at the Theatre Royal, Newcastle, with Bobby Thompson and Leah Bell. I never got to know him well as he used to come into the show after we had started and he invariably left to do a gig before the curtain came down.

However, there was one moment that I still treasure. On the first night of the pantomime, we were all very nervous about how we would be received. Bobby was in the wings, very quiet. I put my arm around him and said: 'Don't worry Bobby, they are going to love you' (even though I had never seen his act.) He looked at me and quietly thanked me. Well, he went on and did 15 minutes, and I've never heard an audience laugh as long or as loud. I stood and watched him, mesmerized, as I did on practically every night of the pantomime.

He was, without doubt, one of the funniest comedians I have ever had the good fortune to work with. He was brilliant.

Aa'm not kiddin' ya, how aa got married into that family aa divvent knaa. They're aal simple.
She's got two brothers... they knaa nowt... they're both working.
And her mother's gannin aroond with one wellington on 'cos the wireless says there's ganna be a foot of snow.

ROY HUDD

Bobby Thompson was a 'one-off' - a provincial comedian in the very best sense. He was so much a part of the North-East. He always said that his act couldn't travel - I disagree. With the Geordie accent being so much better known through a number of television series, I know that he could have travelled.

The last time that I saw him was at the Wimbledon Theatre. The place was packed and he tore the audience apart. He was a genuinely funny man with his own weird view of the world and, whatever the accent, that inspired lunacy came through.

She's telling the neighbours: 'We're going on vacation, Bobby's had a double up - two non-runners.'
She's puttin' sandwiches up on a Wednesday and we're not gannin' till Monday.
Well, ye knaa, tinned tomatoes turn claggy.

Aa brought the wife with is the neet.
She's not very well, she's been breathing.

DAVE NICOLSON -
'THOU'S A FUNNY BUGGER'

My lifelong interest in Bobby Thompson finally culminated in September, 1980, when I approached him for an interview. He asked me what I intended to do with the material and I told him that one day, probably when he was dead, I would write something about him, so it made sense to interview the subject when he was still alive. He laughed at this and said: 'By, thou's a funny bugger,' and invited me to his home in Monkseaton. Our appointment for 9.30am on the following Tuesday came as a surprise to him, as a lady housekeeper went to get him out of bed and remind him of our meeting. He appeared in his back-kitchen about ten minutes later, offered me a cup of tea and admitted that the interview had slipped his mind. He was coughing quite a bit and lit up on a Woodbine to 'clear' his chest into the pail at his side. Sitting there, in his armchair by the fireside, he looked for all the world like a miner who had just finished a shift.

'My childhood was like thousands of others at that time, we didn't have much, but neither did anyone else. I was never badly treated and we always had something to eat and a bed, even if it was shared. I can't remember much about my parents, but my sisters Rosina and Kate did their best for me and I thought a lot of my family.

I don't know why I became a comic - I suppose it was because I like making people laugh and couldn't have stuck at an ordinary job with set hours like a factory or office. I was never much of a scholar, but even when I worked down the pit or in a factory it felt like prison - I was trapped. Entertaining gives me a lot of time for myself. I like to sleep and amuse myself through the day, then I come alive at night.

Apart from my family, I've never had a lot of friends. I've found that when you're up everybody wants you, but when you hit the bottom the same people would cross the road to avoid you. People in this business are selfish because they look over their shoulders all the time. Paddy Fox is my pal - he and his wife Rosie stuck by me, fed me and believed in me when I was on the bottom. They are like family because they don't want anything from me. We have had some great times. Phyllis liked them, Lottie liked them and my lads would do anything for them. Pat Healy and Jeff Holland have been good mates and Joe Ging and Billy Botto helped me when I needed a hand. Professionally, I owe a lot to Richard Kelly for his help and guidance during my early days.

When you are on top, everybody wants you. 'Come on this radio show or this TV show.' 'Appear here for the old people.' I go along with them and speak nicely because in my position you have obligations to the public, but they don't fool me with their soft soap. I do things for charity willingly and will do anything for the Catholic Church in Whitley Bay and the Little Sisters of the Poor - who gave us help as kids with clothes and money. I get annoyed when they expect me to do one charity after another and I'm out of pocket, whereas the so called 'big names' are put up in expensive hotels and chauffeured around.

In this game, it is usually payments in cash and I'm the only entertainer in the North-East who gets a 'pick-up' of my fee before, or just after, my turn. Most have to wait weeks for the money to be paid by the club to their agent and then to them. If clubs don't go along with this arrangement, then I'll not appear and they know it. After all, I put backsides on seats (and they get the money from the public in advance or at the door) so why should I wait for my wages?

What makes me laugh? Generally, very little - except for the old Laurel and Hardy films. Hardly anybody in the business today makes me laugh.

My own act is modelled on Jimmy James and his cigarette. I copied my timing from him. I stand at ease for a purpose. During the laughter, I light my cigarette. As a rule, I give the audience a gag to cause a laugh and then deliver the punch-line, flicking the ash off my cigarette to point the joke. Laurel and Hardy relied essentially on visual gags and I do that in my act. People respond to me and my image which I do not alter. My appearance, without a word spoken, makes them laugh. They would not take to me in a suit: they like to see me in a jersey and old trousers. I play to a cosmopolitan audience and the suit wouldn't go. When I compere, at the Mayfair Ballroom afternoons, I go out in evening dress, but I'm happier with the cap and jumper.

Every night, I put different gags in my act, but I don't change it completely. The audience like something topical, but come to see and hear the act that they know. It suits me fine for, inspite of having a good memory for figures, I've always had difficulty learning and polishing new material.

The centre of my act is poverty. I make poverty the building, the structure for a house and I build around it. There is usually a story to my tag-lines, like the one about Brendan Foster:
'Did you know that Brendan Foster got a medal for doing the 10,000 metres?'
'Why, that's nothing, a bloke in wor street got six months for doing his gas meter.'

What makes me sad? Many things. The cruelty in the world and what people do to each other often makes me cry. I can't stand the ill-treatment of old people or bairns. How anyone can abuse a kid is beyond me.

Fame doesn't amuse me. I do a job of work. Certain aspects are pleasurable, like my records doing well. I am a household name with Geordies and have just come back from playing Doncaster and Coventry to capacity club crowds - mostly Northerners.

I can recall people who came to see me from way back. However, for most of the time, when they come up to me outside, or phone in when I'm on the radio, and ask if I remember so and so in this row or that row, I just say 'certainly' because they feel they know me and it makes them happy. It's the same with all the people who stop you in the street when you're out. Boys come up to me in clubs and say: 'You used to entertain my grandfather,' and I think, great, now you are coming to see me.

I am the oldest Northern comic still working. Now, I can pick and choose what I do, and it is very sweet when I remember at one time begging for work. Television did me a lot of harm. I was not allowed to do what I wanted to do. After the disaster with Tyne Tees TV in 1959, I went through one of the worst periods of my life. There were times when I was ashamed to be seen in a public place. Phyllis had a bad heart and I was drinking very heavily, but she always believed in me and stood by me. This gave me the strength to pull myself together every night and keep going to support my family.

Due to that bad experience with the Tyne Tees TV shows, I made a decision then to do no more television work, other than to go back for the odd appearance on a show. Usually, there is too much rehearsing - even for a guest spot, but Tyne Tees today are very different and always treat me well. I did last week's 'Friday Live' without a rehearsal. They told me that they trusted me and simply sent the car around to collect me. When I am doing certain humour, I visualise that I am playing the part. You've got to get the reaction of the audience. It takes me one minute to size them up. You know by the welcome, when you come out on stage, how you've got to go. The best comedians have a clean brand of humour. I never swear on stage and spend a lot of energy on my concentration.

They wanted me for the 'Cinderella' pantomime (1979/80) at the Theatre Royal, with David Jason and Leah Bell, because they needed someone to draw people in. David Jason was not popular enough to attract people. There were complaints from people who thought that I should not have been there. For that season, I was paid £16,000 for an eight-minute spot in each house, but I did 14 minutes. They wanted my name on the bill.

I would play a week in 'variety' again. You know, the Theatre Royal provides for the society of Newcastle. You'll not find many miners gannin' to the Royal for Shakespeare. To date, I have played the Royal five times. Everybody is very nice now: 'Will you do so and so, and how much do you want?' Now, they allow me to discuss my own money. Oh, yes, aa'm recognised now by people, and I'll be blunt about it, the same people didn't want my company when I was down. They wouldn't look at the side of the road I was on. I treasure my following from the old Grand Theatre in Byker. The true Northerner is the greatest person. They make the greatest audiences. I never thought that I would find the perfect audience, but I did.

With regard to my position now - I don't call it the whip-hand - I call it being popular. I've got a job next Friday night at a dinner, prior to the Durham Miners' Gala. They tell me that Mrs Thatcher is going to be present, but my agent, Brian, and I are looking into that one. They want me to accept a cut in fee because of her presence - it could be a hoax. Aa'm Labour mesel, but she must be a brave woman to face a Labour audience. (Author's note: this was a hoax, although on Bobby or the interviewer I'm not sure.)

You've got to be humble when you go to workingmen's clubs. When I went to the Theatre Royal, the rest of the cast used to push past the crowd at the stage-door with an 'excuse me, please' and head straight for home. I stopped and chatted to them. The man who reached the highest level in the world never reached the sky. Some people say that I'm a star, but I have never thought that way. It's nice for them to think that I'm still the same Bobby Thompson. Never went to my head. I'm pleased at how my career has turned out. What man could go on to ITV or BBC TV, where they normally rehearse between 3.30pm and 9.00pm, without a rehearsal?

I've always liked women, the bigger the better, because you can't beat a good cuddle, son, (wink) and in this game there's no shortage. I like homely women, not the ones who are beautiful, all done up and speak posh. When pretty women ask me if I'll come home with them, I don't go. What do they want with the likes of me? If I wasn't famous they wouldn't even look at me. Phyllis was my wife and best friend... a marvellous woman and mother. I was broken up when she died. Lottie Tate, my housekeeper, who died recently, was also a lovely woman who looked after me and the boys marvellously. Although I'm a bit of a loner, I do get very lonely at times. I have been lucky.

I'm looking for a live-in housekeeper now, but it's hard to find someone who is honest and who is not tied by receiving benefit, which limits how much they can work and earn. Social Security pays people to stay at home, there's a penalty for being honest.

I average around £800 a week and gave up my pension. I have no intention of ever marrying again, but if I did, it would be so that my son, Michael, had a home here after I was gone.

Like most people, I've done some good things in life and some that I'm ashamed of. In this world there's either laughter or despair, especially among poor people, and for me it was never a choice.'

After our interview, which terminated because he had to get up to the betting shop and hadn't washed and changed, he took me into his front room to show me his trophies and photographs. He seemed fondest of two large portraits by Ken Pope, the excellent Newcastle photographer. One was of himself in costume and the other was of Muhammad Ali, which Ken had sent to Ali's Los Angeles home for him to inscribe it to Bobby. We arranged to meet that Saturday at Percy Main Club.

At Percy Main, the place was packed. There was a separate table, near the front, for Bobby's party, which included his fiancée, Mary Douglas (Lottie Tate's sister.) I asked them what they would like to drink and he became offended saying that he would get the drinks. I accompanied him to the bar where people greeted him, and one or two wags, who knew of his teetotal state, loudly offered to buy him a double whisky or brandy. Their offers irritated him. 'They only do that because they know I don't touch the stuff.' I suggested that he get his own back by accepting and giving the drink away to a pensioner, but he said that he couldn't do that in his position. He listened attentively to his singer and then told me afterwards that he preferred weak singers who didn't tell jokes and had cars to give him a lift.

His own spot went down well. You could hear a pin drop until he finished his routine, but when he started to sing the audience started to talk and place their orders. He seemed oblivious to this. I couldn't have been more than twenty seconds following him into the dressing-room, but the costume was off and he was pulling expensive suit trousers over his linings - seriously warning me not to take a photograph. I asked him why, when he wasn't a singer, did he end his act on the weak note of a song and dance that the audience weren't bothered about. He looked at me incredulously and said that it was traditional for a comic to end with a song. When I pursued the matter - that surely an act should end on the highest point - he told me: 'Look, I don't do it for them, I like to sing.'

An official of the club entered and handed him his fee in an envelope. Bobby counted it - £180 as I recall - and then quizzed him about a popular double act (who had played the same club in the previous week) getting over £200. The club man seemed hurt and reassured Bobby that he was the top act and the highest earner. When the man departed, Bobby told me that he did this to keep the clubs on their toes and gauge their reaction when he tackled them. It was just another way of trying to ensure that he received his correct worth in money.

Back at the table, the subject was still payment and he told me that very often he was paid, with his agreement, in kind rather than money - lengths of suiting, food etc. His fiancée, Mary (I wondered whether she knew that he didn't intend to marry), told him to tell me about the stones of fish given to him each month. After some pressing from her, he told me that he received four stone of fish every month from an admirer. 'Well, go on, tell him the rest,' she said.
'What rest?' he asked, getting irritated with her.
'That you don't like fish at all,' she informed. 'And that you give it, or throw it, away.'
'So what?' he said, 'it's given to me, isn't it?'

PHIL PENFOLD - THEATRE CRITIC

I first saw him in 1970 when, as a junior reporter in the North-East, I was told by friends that to get a slice of Geordie life I should go and see Bobby Thompson at a club. I gave in and was spellbound. During his act, you could feel a tidal wave of love from the audience to this little figure. People were mouthing his act with him. It didn't matter to them that they knew his routines so well.

Professionally, he was a classic renegade from the days of variety. Bobby, with his acute social observations, was the Jasper Carrot of his day and his timing for telling jokes was godsent and, in my opinion, on a par with George Burns, Jack Benny, Ken Dodd and Victor Borge.

He turned on like a tap for interviews and was a great wit, but to me he always seemed unsure of himself. Bobby knew his area and never felt comfortable outside of it, but he still underestimated his talent.

Although he led a very ordinary life for a celebrity, offstage he was a bit of an enigma and intensely private. Bobby had his ups and downs, but he was a fighter and Geordies love a fighter.

Our professional paths never crossed a great deal, as he worked mainly in the clubs during the 70s and 80s, except when he did his regular act for the Press Ball, in the theatre for charity shows or the Theatre Royal pantomime, 'Cinderella'.

He was a very astute man and I liked him. Bobby had no illusions or pretensions, which is rare in showbusiness, and this came through in my Radio Newcastle interview with him. I think that Bobby enjoyed our chat on the air and it was certainly one of my most memorable interviews.

Bobby Thompson was the essence of this region and, in my opinion, he did the best that he could with his talent in the North-East. He used to say that his act couldn't travel South. I think that at the time he was right, but since then 'Auf Wiedersehn Pet', 'Spender' and 'Byker Grove' have opened the way for national acceptance of the Geordie accent in entertainment.

You ask me, in view of my reputation as a frank and objective critic, whether or not I would have given The Little Waster a bad review in his own backyard if I though that his performance had warranted it. I can say without hesitation that I would have done so, and Bobby Thompson was too honest to want it any other way.

It's unlucky to go to work the day after ye've been off.

He showed me up all night buying is drink.
Well, I daren't go out the back in case he missed his turn.

CORRINNE WILDE

A few years ago, Bobby Thompson, several artists and I appeared on a special charity show at the City Hall, Newcastle. I was spellbound by his unique style, so much so that I sat down and wrote, with the help of another artiste, Helen Russell, a song about him.

We took the rough draft to him at home for his approval before recording it in a studio. I will never forget the look on his face when he heard it - he shone with delight. He looked up and said: 'It's great, you have it just right, it's really me, hinny.' He thanked us both in a very lovely way and asked what made us write a song about him. I told him he was the best comedian I'd ever seen. I shed a few tears because it was great to see him so happy about our song called "We Love You Bobby T". He said that I was a canny lass and to stay that way. He gave us £5. I told him that I would never spend it, tore it in half and asked him to sign both halves. I gave one half to Helen. He laughed his head off and said it was the only time he had given his autograph on the back of a five pound note. I still have it ten years later and wouldn't part with it for all the tea in China.

We made the record, it turned out well and was played on the local radio. I still have the original photos and some promotion posters. He will never be forgotten.

Aa've had that much corned beef, if anybody cracks a whip aa'm away at a gallop.

MARK LEWIS

The Carousel Club, Chester-le-Street, was where I first met Bobby Thompson, some twenty years ago. I had won a talent contest at the club in 'Search For A Star'. My prize was £100 and a week's booking at the Carousel, playing support to Bobby. It was a great honour for me and it was pleasing that he remembered me after that when we met around the clubs.

When Ronnie Vaughan and I set up the Lewis Vaughan Agency in 1985, we put a mid-week show on at Ashington Universal CIU, which I compered, and Bobby appeared for us. He asked me about our new agency and suggested that, as he wasn't happy with his present situation, he might let us represent him. Naturally, I was enthusiastic, but didn't really expect to hear any more. We were surprised when two or three days later he phoned to say that he would like to join us.

An' she fried two inches of bacon with the rine on. She burnt the b.. bacon. Mind, aa telt her mother, she'll burn no more, aa'll get her a proper grilla. Her mother says: 'Ganna be ne big hairy things runnin around this house.'

RONNIE VAUGHAN

Brian Shelley stabilised Bobby Thompson, really handled him well and rebuilt his reputation for reliability. But Bobby felt neglected when Brian became involved in purchasing pubs and clubs and resented dealing with a secretary. He felt that he was top-class and liked to think that he was the only client. He was still a big name and Mark Lewis and I were delighted to have him on our books as we had only been in the business about eighteen months or so. There was no contract, simply a verbal agreement.

When we first took him over, I think it was early 1985, 1 used to go to 20, Princes Gardens, pick him up and bring him to Blyth. Over a cup of tea, and a bit crack with Mark, I would tell him what was lined up for him, write the details down and then take him back home. After six months, Bobby decided that it was silly to do the round trip so I used to go to his home every Monday morning, just because it was Bobby. Sometimes, he wasn't in a good mood and I'd talk to his son, Michael, but normally he was OK and we would go over his bookings for the week and I'd leave him with all the written details. He had his own arrangements with a taxi firm. We had no difficulties with him turning up, unless he was genuinely ill. He would ring a club to double-check and then tell them: 'OK, bonnie lads, I'll see you at...' He used to phone me a few times a day just to talk - I think he was a lonely man. When I was with him in a club, it really meant a lot to him for young 20-year-old lads to come and say: 'My mother and father told me about you and I came out of curiosity.' He was the only entertainer in Clubland who received his money on the night of the performance. Bobby and the clubs knew that he could put backsides on seats and that he was worth the 'pick-up' arrangement.

Bobby was on our books until his death in 1988, but in those three-and-a-half years demand for him dropped. You have to remember that he was well into his seventies and the co-ordination had left him. Places were filled once on the name, but he was not usually booked again. Bobby knew the score - he could see that there weren't as many tables, and towards the end he could only get a fee of £150. He hated the decline in money and genuinely liked to work as much as possible. Far from happy, he spent many a Saturday and Sunday night in the house because there was no work for him. The act was always off pat, but in the latter days he would start on a story and then drift into another one without finishing. He would go anywhere we booked him. 'How much? £125? £150? Is it a pick-up? Where is it? OK, I'll de it.' Two thirds of the agencies complained that he didn't come up to scratch. It was sad, but still a privilege for us to handle him. We loved his act, but the accent prevented national acclaim. He was, and still is, a legend - there will never be another.

The wife's jealous of me 'cos of the women that runs after me.
Aa was coming out of my hotel the other night when one cheeky looking woman says: 'Hello, handsome, what about £5 for a short time?'
Aa says: 'Aa've nivvor seen £5 for a long time.'

HOMER MICHAELIDES - 'MR HOMER'

Bobby Thompson was first introduced to me in Billy Botto's Club in Byker, Newcastle, in the late Sixties. I think he had regular work there. We met again around 1977, and then our meetings became more regular when he started coming into our Casino Royale Club in Newcastle, a year or so later.

I didn't understand his humour at first - it was like me speaking to him in Greek and him speaking to me in the Geordie language. Often, he used to say to me: 'Did you understand that joke?' and I would tell him that I had not understood a word of it. Gradually, over the years, he would come up and tell me a few jokes slowly and explain them to me. After a while, I began to understand him and his humour.

He came into the casino, not because of who he was, but because he wanted to become a member. He did like his gamble, and would have a flutter on the horses and in the casino. Of course, when he came into the Casino Royale we began to have a great respect for each other. Bobby found that it was a place where, in addition to being well known, he could also make friends. In night-clubs he used to meet people after his show and they wanted to be seen with him. In the casino it was different. Here, it is a members' club where people get to know each other in a very relaxing atmosphere. Once Bobby came into the club, he found that he did not have to protect himself from the public who wanted to sit at his table or have him join them. He told me that in the casino he could find peace and quiet. He could gamble or not gamble as the mood took him. Nobody was forcing him to do anything he didn't want to do. This was the place, he told me, that he could come and relax and let his guard down.

It is amazing the stamina the man had in him, but, of course, he was a night-time person. Some people enjoy the day time from nine until five and the evening is regarded as unsocial hours. With me, and people like Bobby, it is the other way around. Often, I used to see Bobby reach his best as the night was going on.

Bobby made a lot of genuine friends at the casino. Even now, they still talk about him because he was a very affectionate man, a very loving man and an honest man. That is what I know of him. He was friendly with a number of regulars who used to sit and talk with him. He was also a very shy man - people saw him on the stage and thought that he wasn't, but Bobby lived a very shallow life among his own little circle. He often said that he had not travelled more than fifty or sixty miles afield because it was the unknown to him. People here were not after anything from him, only to enjoy a good conversation. He was intelligent, knowledgeable, and very clever, but within limits.

What came out of Bobby was that he was very much a family man. He really loved his sons, Michael and Keith, and always found a way to work them into our conversation. Michael came here a few times and I think Keith did the same, but it was not very often. Many times, he talked to me about his second wife, Phyllis, and the times, in the past, when he had gone through bad experiences as far as his drinking was concerned. He had many regrets about that part of his life, as he felt that his drinking helped to bring him down. After Phyllis died, in the late Sixties, he told me that he never touched a drink. Some people may have thought that he still took a drink, but I can say with certainty that he never touched a drink in the time that I knew him. The most he would ever have was perhaps one tonic water, but his favourite was a nice strong cup of tea, and he would drink tea right through the night. He told me of his sadness when his housekeeper, Lottie Tate, died. She had taken very good care of him and his two sons after Phyllis died. I knew Lottie, but not as well as Cissie - who came on the scene later. Lottie liked to stay at home, but Bobby wanted to go out.

His past reputation for letting people down used to worry him, and other members used to tell me of this old habit. Bobby told me: 'Mr Homer, I used to work for £2 10s a night - that was my living. Really, I used to be worth £5 or £7, but they would use me. Well, if I found a job for £5, it wasn't that I let them down, but I would tell them that I wasn't going to come and do my act for £2 10s.' This used to come out a lot. In the twelve years that I knew the man, I don't think that he let anybody down at all. If there was anything like that, he used to come and see me. I remember once, when he had gone to a job (a night-club somewhere in Durham) and it was snowing so heavily that the taxi had to stop some way from the club. He was unable to walk the remaining distance and he told me that it had been impossible for him to get there. The fact that he had not been able to carry out the booking preyed on his conscience, even though it hadn't been his fault. He told me that he had let them down. That was the only time in my experience, and I knew how much it had bothered him. It used to annoy me to hear people saying: 'Oh, Bobby will let you down.' I told them that this was not the Bobby I knew. In my opinion, it was not that he was greedy over money, he simply knew his own worth.

He spent many, many times with us and most weeks he would be in the casino some six or seven nights. The first thing that he would do would be to come and sit at my table. We would have a chat about how his day had gone, how was his evening, and how he enjoyed the show. Bobby used to love what he was doing. He was a comedian, but he was doing it with a full heart. If he had disliked the venue on a particular night, he would come in and tell me: 'Mr Homer, I will never go to that place again.' He used to tell me that he enjoyed performing his act and that he wanted the people to enjoy what he was doing. If he heard bad language in the clubs, either from another comedian or the public, he told me that he used to get very embarrassed and would stay in his dressing-room so that he didn't have to tolerate it. He always said that he would never appear on a bill with strippers because he had principles, and that was clear to me in the time we were together and saw each other every day. His principles were very, very high - he had respect.

Bobby didn't like clubs where they put him on a bit late and people were intoxicated. He would say that audiences couldn't really appreciate him if they had drunk too much. He liked doing his act in night-spots, but really favoured the workingmen's clubs. Bobby came from a mining village and felt that the type of audience he found in those clubs were his people. He did enjoy a posh club, because he was always an immaculate dresser in direct comparison to his stage costume. Everything was immaculate and matching, and his clothes and shoes had to be spotless. This showed to me that he liked the higher life as well. Right through to the end, he was never anything less than immaculate.

He was a slow player on the tables and could take a long time to lay his bets. This often led to misunderstandings with our other customers who wanted to know why Bobby was allowed to play slowly when they were not allowed to do so. To avoid any misunderstandings, I used to tell Bobby that the casino was required by law to play roulette at a certain speed. When he saw people come to play at the same table as himself, I asked that he move away quietly to another one so that he didn't distract other players. People thought that he was gambling a lot, but it wasn't really a lot because he was laying and taking odds on the table. He would lay quite a few chips, but you can cover the whole of the table (roulette has thirty-six numbers and one zero, making it thirty-seven) by putting on thirty-seven chips and you will only lose one chip. As you can appreciate, he got his entertainment quite cheaply.

Roulette was definitely his game. He would play blackjack occasionally, but didn't enjoy it in the same way. Although he was a slow player, he found that blackjack was even too slow for him. Maybe the reason behind his enjoyment of roulette was because it reminded him of horse-racing. Something like thirty-seven horses running there, and the speed they were running was similar to the wheel going around - perhaps that was the fascination for him. Of course, roulette is different from other games. If you are down and you hit your numbers, you can soon recover because the odds are greater. As I said earlier, he played small amounts on several numbers, that is why he could last so long and at the end his losses would not be great. He always played and paid in cash and it would be wrong of me to say how much he gambled each night.

Many times, we talked about him going abroad and travelling to Cyprus, my homeland, but his fear was flying. He would say 'yes' to visiting Cyprus, but as the time got nearer he would say that it may be too hot for him. His favourite holiday resort was Blackpool and he went there for many years to the same hotel. The farthest he travelled was when he went down to London to appear on the Wogan show and they put him up in the Waldorf Hotel. Of course, the Waldorf to Bobby was strange. When he came back, he told me: 'Oh, Mr Homer, at the Waldorf we didn't need to take our towels or soap. There were so many towels there and they had so many soaps.' One afternoon at the Waldorf, he and Cissie, his wife, sat down to have afternoon tea. If I remember rightly, he said the bill for a pot of tea, a sandwich and a piece of cake was £6-£7.50. He told me that he was shocked and didn't know whether he had bought the crockery as well. This was Bobby all over and, of course, he was talking a lot about the Waldorf because he was not used to it. But he made a joke about it, and even if the joke was against himself he would say it without feeling that he was too big to do so. Other people might have covered up about it, and pretended that they were used to it, not Bobby. His food was plain English food and he wanted nothing extravagant. Sometimes, I would try to persuade him to choose something from the menu here, but he would say: 'Oh, don't tell me about this or that, I don't know what they are.' With us, in the casino, the most he would ever have would be his egg-and-chips or toast and marmalade and his pot of tea.

Never, over all the years of out friendship, did I give him a penny. I say this because some people have said that I must have paid him to be in the casino. No, there was a genuine friendship between us. There was mutual respect and, of course, we really didn't need to have Bobby sit in the casino every night to bring the punters in. But a lot of the time people misunderstood. They would see Bobby getting his tea, but we run a place where members have their free buffets and meals - we run promotions.

We used to talk about money. I told him he wouldn't always be healthy enough to work and should save a little. In Bobby's last years, his health was not as good as people thought and, although he was still in demand, often he wasn't up to accepting the jobs. He told me that at his age he wasn't worried about money as he had his little house and didn't want anything from anyone. He wasn't a greedy man - he wanted the rate for

191

the job, but once he got a fair rate he put his heart into his work.

It was clear to me from our talks that he wasn't able to look after his affairs or finances. When the tax-man came after him, it was a shock to him to be told that he owed that amount of money. He told me that he didn't have the money, he had never had that money. Of course, I didn't know the details of his affairs, but I know that the tax business bothered him very much in the last few years, even though he used to joke about it as part of his act. He used to sit down and tell me that he had received a letter from the tax-man, but he would not show it to anybody else. Despite the jokes that he was making, he was an honest man who never wanted to owe anybody a penny and he felt very bad about the tax demands. I think something in him cracked towards the end and may have put him down, because over the last three or four years he wasn't doing that much work, he was not a well man. I could tell that he was going down and down.

A point I would like to make is about his charity work. Some people used to say that he didn't do a lot for charity. I used to get very annoyed when I heard remarks like that. I used to suggest that perhaps they were not approaching the man in the right way. I told them, perhaps you are wanting the man to give up one night's work, maybe on his most demanding nights of the week like a Friday or Saturday, without even being prepared to offer him anything, because you say it's for charity.

From my experience, he never wanted anything out of charity for himself, but Bobby wasn't a wealthy man and he could only make a living from his performances. What used to annoy him was the treatment afforded to other artists by promoters of big charity shows. Artists would be brought all the way from London (sometimes, they would even have a previously arranged booking in the area) or anywhere in the country. The organisers would pay their air fares or first-class rail travel, put them into a five-star hotel (all expenses paid) and transport them in a chauffeured Rolls Royce. This treatment cost a fortune. However, when it came to Bobby they used to say: 'Oh, well, Bobby won't do it for nothing.' But they weren't even prepared to meet some of his expenses.

Once, when I sent forty handicapped children to a sports competition at the Stoke Mandeville Hospital, Bobby came down to the casino in the morning to wave them off. When they returned to see me (some with gold medals) a few days later, he came again to greet them. He was always willing to do anything for charity - but when they wouldn't even offer him something towards his expenses, he told me that he would not let people take him for a fool. He used to say that even if they gave him a hundred pounds - the cost of a night's hotel for the other artists - he didn't mind.

We did a charity television piece together, in the Assembly Rooms, for Channel Four. They televised Bobby and myself doing a Greek dance. However, when it was shown, if you blinked you missed the dance sequence. I wrote to the TV company to see if they would sell me the unused footage, but they never replied.

He cared about people and day-to-day life. People were an enjoyment to him. He used to enjoy sitting, watching and assessing people's characters. For all I knew my customers, he knew them in his way very well, even though he didn't speak to some of the members. He would tell me to look at this one or that one, and what they were doing or what was going on at such and such a table. He was a very alert man, but his outlook on life was not a demanding one... he didn't want very much out of life.

Sometimes, he brought an old lady and her daughter to the casino when he came with Cissie. The old lady (Mrs Parks, I think) must have been about eighty-five or ninety. He told me that she used to run a corner shop near Princes Gardens and had been kind to him when he had nothing. It gave him great pleasure to bring the old lady out and he used to tell me how much she looked forward to her visits.

Another person he brought along as a guest was the best man, Ken Pendleton, from his wedding to Cissie. Of course, when he decided to marry Cissie, I think I was the first one to know about it. Bobby had a chat with me and told me about his wedding plans. He asked me what I thought of Cissie, as I had seen her here a few times. Well, I couldn't see anything wrong in her and I thought she would be a good wife to him. This is an example of the respect we had for each other.

Paddy Fox was a good friend of Bobby's, a real nice man, and they thought the world of each other. It was a real friendship, but for Bobby it was like having a friend who was there to do everything for you - like a butler or a valet. Paddy was there for anything Bobby wanted, and it used to give Bobby pleasure to bring Paddy out with him. Bobby was always thankful for anything that people did for him - that extended to his taxi driver or anyone. My staff would let him know immediately when his taxi arrived. Sometimes, when he was sitting down talking to me and didn't want to jump straight up, he would ask them to invite the driver into the club to have a coffee in reception. He wasn't the kind of man who would turn round and say that as the taxi driver gets paid, he should stay outside and wait. He would keep checking to ask if the driver was all right.

Cissie accompanied him on many occasions and they always seemed very happy. When they were in the casino, she was always very protective towards him. If anybody dared to upset Bobby, Cissie would rush to deal with it, and she was always on the look out in case anybody pushed him accidentally at a table or anything like that. She would always open his sugar, put it in his tea and stir it up for him. She would butter his toast and put the marmalade on. Often, I would say: 'Bobby, nothing to do?' and he would tell me that he would not know where to start buttering his toast or sugaring his tea. They always came here together and seemed very happy.

Even during the last years, he would still come to the casino nearly every night, although some nights he wouldn't gamble - or maybe just ten, twenty or thirty pounds. Of course, being a regular in a casino, or being a gambler, doesn't mean you are losing every day. You have your winnings as well. After all, the casino has only 2.3 per cent in its favour on each spin. Over the year, he may have lost £1,000 or £1,500 or £2,000 - some people will have spent that amount on their drinking at ten and twenty pounds a week. So, the man was not drinking, but the gambling was part of his entertainment. He was very comfortable here. He used to say to me that he had two homes - one where he went to sleep, another home when he came here to relax and see his friends.

During the last period of his life, he was sick for one or two weeks and I was away at the time. On the night I came back, I arrived at the casino about 9.30pm and they asked me if I knew that Bobby was in hospital. I asked where he was - he was in Preston Hospital, North Shields. At around ten or eleven the same evening, I took my son, Anthony, and we went to the hospital. We went into a private room. He had his two sons there with him, holding his hands. That was the first thing I saw when I went into the room.

Keith said to Bobby: 'Well, we told you Mr Homer would come and see you.' Apparently, he had been asking for me for some days. I walked to his bed. He looked near to death, but lifted himself off the bed about nine inches, looked at me and we shook hands.

I said to him: 'Bobby, what are you doing here. Come on, up you get, we are going to the casino.' He managed to put a slight smile on his face for one or two minutes as he held himself up - then he just lay back. I stayed there twenty minutes to half an hour. I had a little chat to the boys, but, of course, Bobby couldn't speak to me. He was looking at me without being able to express or say anything, but the expression I could see showed me just how much he thought of me. It must have been around half-past eleven when I left. His boys were still there with him. I said to my son, as we were leaving, that we would be losing Bobby very quickly. Within an hour, one of his sons phoned to tell me that he had passed away. I was sad, but pleased that I had gone to see him, even at the last moments. I believe, apart from his two sons, I must have been the last person to see him before he died.

I only knew Bobby in the casino. It was sad that the only time I went to his house was on the day of his funeral. On this sad occasion, Cissie very kindly offered me a large photograph which Bobby had always said was for Mr Homer, if he wants it. To me this was a great honour, particularly as Bobby had wanted me to have it. I found a nice place for it in the television room of the casino, where people still come to see it when they talk or ask about him. I tell them: 'Look, he is ready to speak to you.'

People have come to me and said that he died a poor man, and asked where did all of his money go to! After all, wasn't he here gambling six or seven nights a week! I would say to them that in his last few years he stopped making money. He was a very fragile man and had the expense of a taxi wherever he went, and what I have discovered is that people in the night-clubs used to ask him for money. He felt that by giving them that fiver, tenner or twenty pounds he was helping them, but a lot of people took advantage of that kindness and a lot of money went in that way.

In some ways, he never got the true recognition that he deserved. He got the recognition from his audiences, the ordinary people in the clubs, because he was very well supported. However, I think a lot more could have been done, and should have been done, by the local councils. As someone from outside the area, it was clear to me that he was somebody who kept the dialect and area culture going. Now, people are trying to bring back Bobby's jokes and again it is sad that a man dies before people can see how good he really was.

How are yaa?
Holidays are ower, ain't they? Some debt left.
Aa cannit sleep for debt, aa'm up to there.
Aa wish aa was a bit taller.

Her mother was on the gin an' aa was toppin' it up wi' domestos.
She wasn't drunk, but her hair turned yellow.

'You didn't laugh when aa was fightin' for ya.

Anybody can laugh when it's ower.'